Classics of Design

Classics of Design

Hilary Beyer & Catherine McDermott

REFERENCE GROUP
Brown

ISBN 1 84044 101 1

Produced by:
The Brown Reference Group
8 Chapel Place
Rivington Street
London EC2A 3DQ, UK
www.brownpartworks.co.uk

Editors: Dawn Titmus, Diana Craig
Designer: Reg Cox
Picture Researcher: Susannah Jayes
Editorial Director: Lindsey Lowe
Art Director: Dave Goodman
Production Manager: Matt Weyland

The authors would like to thank Edmund Whitworth for his additional research work

Contents

Introduction

In 1936 the German-born architectural historian Nikolaus Pevsner wrote *The Pioneers of Modern Design*, an important survey of design that is still widely read. The book was essentially a survey of design development from the Industrial Revolution to the Modern Movement. Pevsner believed the expanding world of industrial consumer goods was an evolutionary process, a progressive development from the experiments of the early 19th century toward a pinnacle of achievement he identified in the work of Mies van der Rohe, Walter Gropius and Marcel Breuer, a trio of distinguished architects whom Tom Wolfe was famously to describe as "White Gods" in his book *From Bauhaus To Our House* (1981). *The Pioneers of Modern Design* was a landmark publication reflecting a widely held belief in industrial production, new materials, and new forms for the 20th century. In effect, it began a publishing trend for design books that helped the reader to understand something of the way design had shaped the modern world.

The early years of the 20th century witnessed great changes in production, taste, and consumer demand. The period saw the development of the second great Industrial Revolution, often called the era of "The Machine Age," of cars, telephones, cinema, new materials, and new technologies. In the developed world it set in place the industrial framework and culture that has led to the third major revolution of the modern world, structured around the information technologies of cell phones and personal computers, the impact of which we are still coming to terms with. Our view of design in the 21st century reflects these profound changes and are rather different from those of the last century. Design and consumer products are now widely seen as a way of expressing individual identity and of satisfying personal needs and desires. The cult of the object is reflected in the multiplicity of design shops and retail outlets, and the burgeoning growth of museums and exhibitions that explore contemporary design.

The 84 design classics described in this book reflect that diversity of approach and include objects ranging from a robotic toy to a juke box. It is a compilation that tries to offer information not only about the history of design, but also about the history of taste and of social and technological change. One of the early entries is a late design from the founding father of the Arts and Crafts Movement, William Morris, whose work and writings led to a revival in craft production and reflected his century's exploration of surface decoration and pattern. Naturalist forms provided the starting point for Morris's creations, and at the turn of the century Art Nouveau represented the last flowering of a 19th-century decorative style; works such as the Tiffany Dragonfly Lamp embraced sinuous, naturalistic forms typically derived from exotic animal life. In the 20th century, the Modern Movement challenged the supremacy of decoration in design but it never really went away, finding different expressions in each decade, from the Art Deco interior of Radio City in New York to the exuberance of Pop Art design, and, more recently, as an important element in the work of the legendary Italian designer Ettore Sottsass.

From the early 1920s, the new exponents of Modernism offered an aesthetic that emphasized mass-production techniques, new materials such as tubular steel, plywood, and heat-resistant glass, and a restricted palette of colors. For the teachers and students of the Bauhaus—the most influential creative school of the 20th century—design could be reduced to the following formula: a series of geometric forms—the circle and square for objects designed for industrial production—and the use of a restricted palette, with an emphasis on the primary colors. Gerrit Rietveld's Red/Blue Chair represents one of the earliest experiments to define this new approach, and was followed by the tubular steel furniture of Marcel Breuer and Mies van der Rohe, Marianne Brandt's lamps and lighting, and Wilhelm Wagenfeld's kitchenware. Although interrupted by World War II, this Modernist ideology was deeply influential in shaping the world of consumer goods and we can read its influence in objects such as Bellini's Olivetti typewriter and in the work of contemporary designers such as Jasper Morrison.

Other powerful social and cultural forces came into play following World War II. The postwar economic revival of the United States and Europe put pressure on designers to develop new styles in ways that offered a more playful agenda, offering color and fun. The theories and ideas of Pop Art introduced imagery and styling from popular culture—witness the throwaway Blow Chair—complemented by a fascination with new materials, as demonstrated by Robin Day's colorful plastic stacking chair of the mid-1960s.

In the late 1960s, the emergence of the more inclusive agenda of Postmodernism started to break down traditional hierarchies. In the new world of goods the values of a Barbie doll could be discussed alongside those of the Coca-Cola bottle or a Chanel perfume bottle. The Modernist hardline agenda didn't go away; it ran alongside this search for the new and the different. However, emerging designers brought humor as well as functionality to their creations, a development reflected here in such objects as Alessi's products, the lemon squeezer by Philippe Starck, and the anthropomorphic forms of Venturini's sugar sifters and Julian Brown's elephant tape dispenser.

The biggest agenda for design in the 21st century is the challenge of new technologies, the growth of personal communication devices, computers, and miscellaneous related gadgets. Included alongside the established design classics on the following pages, you will find the hand-held Game Boy by Nintendo, cell phones by Nokia, and laptops by Apple, in which design acts as the interface between the new technological revolution and the way we apply its advances to our lives. Quality and excellence in design of contemporary objects is still highly valued—witness the widespread praise for Jonathan Ive's extraordinary achievements for Apple. Such work suggests that we still look to celebrate the world of design today, however unfamiliar its face might appear to late 19th-century pioneers such as William Morris.

Catherine McDermott

Campbell's Soup Can

The commercial world of packaging and advertisements became a popular subject matter for artists with the development of pop art in the 1960s. Pop artists such as Richard Hamilton in Britain and Roy Lichtenstein in America took the references one stage further and made popular imagery the subject matter of their paintings. The American artist Andy Warhol belongs to this group, and he became fascinated by the repetition that followed mass-production and packaging. His painting *200 Campbell's*

Above: Campbell's soup is as good as homemade, suggests this advertisement.

Soup Cans in 1962 immortalized this can, and elevated the art of packaging by encouraging a closer look at the subtle differences between different cans. Like so many of Warhol's themes, the painting made reference to his own life and experience, and turned the everyday into an iconic image that represented American culture.

The soup was first canned by Joseph Campbell in 1869 when he started his food-canning factory in New Jersey. Soup was, and is, a successful convenience food because the flavor is not drastically altered in the canning process. The stroke of genius with this label, left, was that it gave a particular product a clear identity on the grocery shelf, which distinguished it from similar products of similar quality.

The designer of the label is not known, but the division of the label space into red and white bands with several different typefaces and sizes has been used on products ever since. In this case, the designer added an important-looking coat of arms. The apparently handwritten logo, which was also used by the equally famous Coca-Cola bottle, was established at this early stage to make the product familiar and recognizable.

Willow Wallpaper

William Morris

Willow Wallpaper

1875

William Morris 1834–1896

British

William Morris was one of the dominant figures of late 19th-century design. The founding father of what became known as the Arts and Crafts Movement, he was not only a design writer but also a socialist activist, poet, and, arguably, the greatest pattern designer of his generation. He founded the firm Morris, Marshall, Faulkner & Co. in 1861, 10 years after London's Great Exhibition of 1851. The mass-produced, machine-made objects exhibited there seemed to him to have degraded the originals, built by craftsmen, that they were imitating. He wanted to return to the idea of the artist as craftsman, and when he eventually set up his own workshop it consisted of his artist and designer friends as well as superb artisans. They produced wallpapers, furniture, tapestries, stained glass, carpets, and furnishing materials, and developed the Kelmscott Press, founded in 1890, to raise the standard of book design and printing.

There was some degree of contradiction in this revolutionary socialist's ideas and aspirations. On the one hand, Morris wanted his objects to be accessible to everyone to enrich their everyday lives but, on the other hand, his beautifully produced designs were more expensive and exclusive than most people could afford. However, the quality and aesthetics of his work did leave a lasting impression that has filtered down to the products we buy today, which can be produced by less expensive processes.

The willow wallpaper takes the motif of the willow tree as its inspiration. Morris produced the design on paper, and it was printed in his workshop—he was not against the idea of craftsmen recreating another artist's original ideas. With its mixture of soft greens, it has a simpler theme than many of his other wallpapers, which more resemble tapestries with their elaborate trellises of flowers and birds, and which have color combinations that required many printing plates. Willow wallpaper continues to be made by Sanderson, the English wallpaper company, and fits well into modern interiors despite the changes in the design of furniture and fittings since Morris's day.

Kettle with Stand and Burner

Christopher Dresser

Kettle with Stand and Burner

1878–1879

Christopher Dresser
1834–1904

British

Christopher Dresser was arguably the first professional industrial designer, and his distinctive vision remains a model and inspiration for subsequent generations. He belongs to the 19th-century arts and crafts tradition of the time, although, unlike his contemporary William Morris, he believed in engaging with machine production.

Dresser originally trained as a botanist but later turned his attention to design. He combined his rational scientific training with the 19th-century preference for decorative forms. His rational approach produced many startling modern forms and shapes that illustrate his theories of fitness for purpose and a quest for principles of design.

Dresser worked in many different materials, including metal—especially silver and electroplated silver, such as this example—and pottery, glass, and textiles. He essentially operated as a freelance consultant for any manufacturing company that would pay him, such as metalworkers Hukin and Heath of Birmingham and London. In 1879 he set up the Linthorpe Pottery in Middlesborough, England, in association with businessman John Harrison. Later Dresser produced designs for a Scottish glass manufacturer in Glasgow, and much of his output was sold—under the trade name Clutha—to the fashionable London department store Liberty. Dresser's visually startling designs in metalware are only one part of his design output, but they remain his best-known work. It is no surprise that the Italian firm Alessi decided to reproduce a range of his early designs, including this kettle and cruets, for a contemporary marketplace.

Dresser's kettle has the characteristic ebonized bar handle that derives its shape from Japanese bamboo handles. The design adheres to his theory that the handle and spout "should form a right-angle through the center of gravity, so that the weight of the vessel is well balanced during pouring." The angular shape with the weight firmly at the bottom, the straight, sharply angled spout, and the way the piece fits neatly on to its stand all combine to make Dresser's kettle wholly fit for its purpose.

Swiss Army Knife

Carl Elsener

The knife that was first developed for the Swiss Army as a multipurpose "Soldier's knife" originally contained two blades, a can opener, corkscrew, and a punch, and became known as the Swiss Army Knife. Designed using the colors of the national Swiss flag, the knife's bright red body and Swiss white cross give it a distinct design identity. It was the invention of Carl Elsener, and the patent taken out was named Victorinox after his mother Victoria.

The knife's functional system for pulling out the tools and high-quality sharp blades from the body reflected the tradition of Swiss expertise in precision tools and engineering. The quality, versatility, and compactness of the design ensured a much wider market for the knife, however. Four generations of the family have continued to produce the Swiss Army Knife and safeguard its reputation for quality production.

Today there are as many as a hundred different versions of the knife and more evolve as time goes on. They vary from the Bijou, a knife for the handbag, to the SwissChamp model, which is a veritable tool kit, containing—in addition to a choice of blades—a corkscrew, can and bottle openers, nail file, screwdrivers, wood saw, pliers, scissors, toothpick, and chisel. It has become a legendary object that is used by people in every situation from the mundane to the heroic—from horse riders who still find the hoofpick attachment effective for removing stones from horses' hooves, to a climber on Everest who used it to unblock oxygen pipes.

The development of the Swiss Army Knife was a reflection of the Victorian interest in small, portable inventions, rather similar to the current vogue for miniaturization. Part of the knife's enduring popularity can be attributed to consumers' continuing love of gadgets. Today the Swiss Army Knife is not merely a fashion accessory and a fun gadget, but it also retains a powerful image as the adventurer's essential compact tool kit that fits neatly and conveniently into the pocket.

Dragonfly Tiffany Lamp

Louis Comfort Tiffany

Louis Comfort Tiffany was one of the first American designers not only to be inspired by but also to lead the European Art Nouveau movement. He was the son of Charles Lewis Tiffany, founder of Tiffany & Co., the well-known and fashionable New York department store selling elaborate silverware.

Louis Tiffany trained as a painter and turned to interior decoration in 1879. He became fascinated by the potential of colored glass, and he employed chemists to research formulas for new colors and effects such as opalescence, iridescence, and molding techniques. At the 1889 International Exhibition in Paris he saw the new glass techniques being developed by French designers such as Émile Gallé and Ernest Baptise Leveillé. At that time he met the entrepreneur and collector Samuel Bing, who was a leading dealer in works of art from the Far East and owned an Art Nouveau gallery and shop in Paris.

In 1892 Tiffany formed the Tiffany Glass and Decorating Company (renamed Tiffany Studios in 1900). The first Tiffany glass factory opened in 1893 at Corona, Long Island. Tiffany had strong connections with companies and artists in Europe, such as Bing's famous outlet in Paris, and Tiffany glass won prizes in international exhibitions. He produced decorative colored glass panels for architectural interiors, and Tiffany lamps became an essential component of every fashionable interior.

This Dragonfly lamp has a leaded glass shade over a gilt bronze base. Its themes of nature and organic forms recall the European Art Nouveau style. The bases were adapted for electric power, and the colors and techniques were developed to complement the brighter light. Bing introduced the lamp to Europe in his Paris outlet, and it was among some of the original electric lamps that were first shown by him in England. Since the 1960s there have been several revivals of Tiffany glass, with many cheap imitations, and they are still found in modern minimalist interiors.

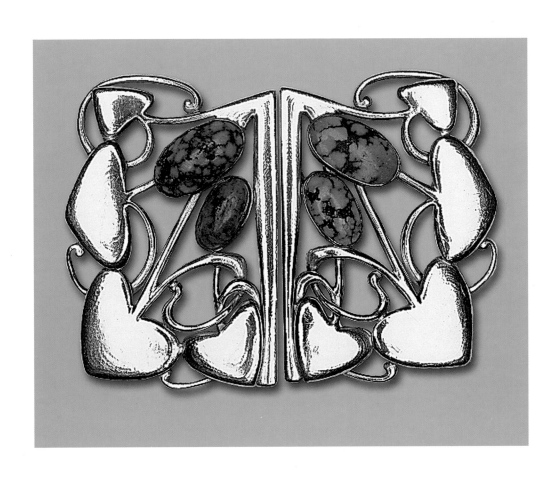

Silver Buckle

Archibald Knox

Archibald Knox was part of a generation of British architects and designers at the end of the 19th century who established British design at the cutting edge of the avant-garde. He was a member of the British Arts and Crafts movement, which sought to develop a new, modern, and more restrained alternative to the style known as Art Nouveau in continental Europe. Knox's designs for silverware that he produced at the turn of the century are recognizably of that time.

Knox spent his early working life on the Isle of Man, and became fascinated by the Celtic interlacing patterns he saw firsthand there, which he often combined with the motifs from nature associated with Art Nouveau. When Knox moved to London in 1897 to teach at art schools, including Kingston College of Art, he began to work as a freelance designer for the famous London department store, Liberty & Co.

Knox was most probably introduced to Liberty by his friend and tutor, the architect M. H. Baillie Scott, whom he met on the Isle of Man and who had designed for Liberty from 1893. Knox's association with Liberty became his most famous collaboration, and he designed a whole series of silver jewelry, pewter ware, and domestic objects for the store. This range included Cymric silverware, which was manufactured by the firm W. H. Haseler of Birmingham, England. Liberty never named its designers at that time, and Haseler was later registered as Liberty & Co. Cymric Ltd. The range, which included tableware and jewelry, was very successfully marketed.

This silver buckle combines the Celtic influences favoured by Knox with the tendrils and plant forms that typify Art Nouveau. The four ovals in the center are enameled in blue, and the relief interlacing patterns are simple and complement the overall shape elegantly without becoming too elaborate. Knox's ability to reflect the spirit of his age was combined with a modern ability to work with materials and maintain proportion, which ensured that his work has remained popular and timeless.

Ladderback Chair

Charles Rennie Mackintosh

Ladderback Chair

c. 1903

Charles Rennie Mackintosh
1868–1928

British

Charles Rennie Mackintosh has become one of the most famous architects of the 20th century. His distinctive style is closely associated with the Art Nouveau movement, which started in the 1880s. It was a fresh look at design that responded to the natural forms of plants and the whiplash curve, which was a dominant feature of the movement. Its free, asymmetric shapes introduced a new aesthetic whose ideas spread throughout Europe, developing in France and Germany almost simultaneously.

Mackintosh designed his buildings and all the parts inside to produce a detailed, total look. The furniture and fittings in the rooms were given space to "speak," and their clear outlines were often set against white walls. His desire for clarity did not preclude decoration, though, and he worked with his wife, Margaret, whose decorative panels, stencils, and textiles were incorporated into private houses and into the Willow Tea Rooms he designed in Glasgow, Scotland. In his famous Glasgow School of Art building, he enlivened the stark verticals and high rooms with decorative features carefully calculated to articulate the shapes and complement the whole.

This ladderback chair was specifically designed for Hill House in Helensburgh, Scotland, built in 1902–1905 for the publisher Walter Blackie. It appears in the bedroom, where it functions as a space marker against the white wall. The chair has an ebonized ashwood frame, with an upholstered seat in fabric that was originally green on pink. Mackintosh's chairs have been criticized for being impractical, but this bedroom chair was not just decorative—it was also functional for its purpose: practicality and detail were vital to Mackintosh, and he paid careful attention to the lives and needs of his clients.

Like many of Mackintosh's pieces of furniture, this chair has been reproduced by the Italian furniture company Cassina. It fits perfectly into modern minimalist interiors, as well as contrasting with the Art Nouveau designs that are still popular today.

Wine Glasses

Josef Hoffmann

Josef Hoffmann was born in Pirnitz, which is now part of the Czech Republic. He studied architecture first in Brno, then under Otto Wagner at the Vienna Academy, Austria. He had a prolific career as an architect and designer, and became one of the most influential voices in design and architecture in the first half of the 20th century, running teaching courses from 1899–1936. From 1896–1897 he worked in Wagner's studio, and then in 1897 co-founded the radical Vienna Secession group with artist Gustav Klimt, designer Koloman Moser, and fellow architect Joseph Maria Olbrich. He took part in the International Exhibitions in Paris and Vienna at the beginning of the century and, with Koloman Moser, founded the Wiener Werkstätte, which was a successor to the British Arts and Crafts movement, the aim of which was to promote "an intimate relationship between the public, the designer, and the craftsman, and to create good, simple things for the home."

Hoffmann's design aesthetic is clearly expressed in the Palais Stoclet (1905–1911) in Brussels, Belgium, which was built for a Belgian financier living in Vienna, and was to be a luxurious palace of the arts—part museum, part house for entertaining. Its large, complicated elevation is balanced but asymmetric, rising to a stepped stair tower. The facade has thin, stone-slab veneers and linear moldings emphasizing the verticals, with the horizontals of the different levels marked out. The grid pattern around the arched windows serves to highlight the play of horizontal to vertical.

These handblown glasses represent a different side of Hoffman's work, and were made to his design by Austrian glass manufacturer Lobmeyr, who belonged to the Wiener Werkstätte. Their shapes and linear decoration are characteristic of his formal aesthetic, respecting the transparency of glass and emphasizing the shape with simple decoration. Their appeal was international and spread to the United States, where Wiener Werkstätte products became fashionable in the first half of the 20th century.

Same Difference.

Funny thing about Coca-Cola. The bottle is different today. But inside? Coke has the same great taste. Unchanged since 1886. Which was when things first started to go better. Talk about having a taste you never get tired of! After 81 years...

Coke still has the taste you never get tired of.

Coca-Cola Bottle

Coca-Cola

Coca-Cola Bottle

1915

Coca-Cola

American

Coca-Cola have always understood the value of this shapely glass bottle, which is still used in limited numbers alongside the more popular cans and plastic bottles. The company have always guarded the value of their brand image. An advertisement from the 1960s shows President J. F. Kennedy with a Coke bottle, about which the American pop artist Andy Warhol commented in 1975, "You can be watching TV and see Coca-Cola and you can know that the president drinks Coke, Liz Taylor drinks Coke, and just think, you can drink Coke too."

The original Coca-Cola syrup was invented by Dr. John Pemberton, a pharmacist in Atlanta, Georgia, in 1886. A year later Willis Venables, a drugstore barman, mixed the syrup with soda water and sold it by the glass. All rights to the product were bought by an American businessman Asa Griggs Candler in 1891, and the drink continued to be sold in soda fountains until it was bottled in 1894. The legend is that Pemberton had asked his bookkeeper, Frank Robinson, to create the famous handwritten trademark.

In 1915 a Swedish engineer, Alex Samuelson, of the Root Glass Company of Terre Haute, Indiana, started work on the curved bottle design, which, it was claimed, was based on an illlustration of a cocoa bean found in a copy of the *Encyclopaedia Britannica*. The first bottles went into production in 1916. The distinctive shape has been altered and refined over the years, and in 1955 French designer Raymond Loewy was commissioned to slenderize the bottle's curves.

During World War II, Coca-Cola pledged to provide limitless supplies to the American troops for the same price that they paid at home, and a network of bottling plants was set up, ensuring Coke's worldwide availability. An internationally recognizable icon, Coke's secret drink formula, distinctive packaging, and marketing have ensured its continued undisputed global lead in the soft-drinks market.

Red/Blue Chair

Gerrit Thomas Rietveld

Red/Blue Chair

1918

Gerrit Thomas Rietveld
1888–1964

Dutch

Architect Gerrit Thomas Rietveld's Red/Blue chair remains the first radical new design that was to define the design aesthetic of the 20th century. It is interesting to note that the chair, the name of which is simply defined by its color, started out in 1917 as a black chair in which the dimensions and specifications were constantly adjusted. It was not until 1923—when Rietveld had become influenced by Dutch painters Piet Mondrian and Theo van Doesburg—that the color was introduced.

In 1919 Rietveld became a member of the De Stijl group of artists and architects, whose aim was to break down divisions between fine and applied arts and to create new and pure forms of architecture and art. Mondrian, for example, refined the group's palettes to the primary colors with simple tones, and its forms to straight verticals and horizontals. The Red/Blue chair can now be seen as a three-dimensional version of this aesthetic, with the clear colors defining both the solids and the voids between them.

Members of the De Stijl group searched for a universal form of expression whose message could be realized in everything, "including the everyday things of life." Rietveld trained in his father's cabinet-making shop, and always retained a practical approach, exploring his ideas with prototypes made in cardboard and wood. For Rietveld, the Red/Blue chair reflected his search for an original object with no trace of the human hand—a search for objectivity and anonymity. He went on to explore these ideas and pure form in his famous Schröder House (1924–1925) in Utrecht, the Netherlands, which, with his chair and other items of furniture, influenced architecture and design for the rest of the 20th century.

This chair's construction is clearly expressed and ingeniously assembled, so that the person sitting on it can appear to be floating. It has been reproduced widely ever since it first appeared—by students studying the De Stijl group and by Italian furniture company Cassina in a successful relaunch of it in the 1970s.

N° 5 - GARDENIA - CUIR DE RUSSIE - N° 22 - BOIS DES ILES

N°5

CHANEL

PARIS

THE MOST TREASURED NAME IN PERFUME

CHANEL

Chanel No. 5 Bottle

Gabrielle "Coco" Chanel

Chanel No. 5 Bottle

1921

Gabrielle "Coco" Chanel
1883–1971

French

Gabrielle "Coco" Chanel was one of the first fashion designers to realize the value of producing a range of perfumes to market alongside the clothes. Her chief parfumier, Ernest Beaux, is reputed to have given her a number of perfumes from which to choose for this first, important scent. She chose No. 5—a blend of jasmine, rose, ylang-ylang, iris, sandalwood, and vetiver, with the addition of a synthetic ingredient called aldehyde to enhance the aromas—and decided to retain this as its name since the perfume was distinctive enough to need no further description.

Chanel kept a legendary control on all the activities of her fashion house and her creative director, Jacques Helleu. Helleu noted that she designed this bottle herself, based on a toiletry bottle in a man's travel set she owned, made by Charvet the jeweler. Before the arrival of No. 5, the tradition within the perfume industry had been to create voluptuous, ornate bottles that expressed the nature of the perfume. However, Chanel saw the advantage of a simple yet distinctive shape that drew its inspiration from the modernist move toward minimal geometric forms.

Chanel knew that other designers would follow her lead, and her shrewd marketing sense ensured No. 5's plentiful supply stood up to the competition. In 1924 she appointed the Frenchman Pierre Wertheimer, co-owner of Bourjois cosmetics, to produce the perfume in a new company called Parfums Chanel, with Beaux as its first technical director. From 1921 to 1970, Chanel continued to supervise the subtle development of the bottle's square-cornered, chunky shape. Despite the original aim to make it expensive and inimitable, Chanel No. 5 became affordable, and glamorous devotees such as Marilyn Monroe boosted its enormous sales. Its status as a 20th-century design icon was ensured in 1985 when pop artist Andy Warhol produced 10 screen prints of it called *No. 5*, and the perfume joined the ranks of Coca-Cola, Brillo, and Campbell's soup as one of the most famous products of the 20th century.

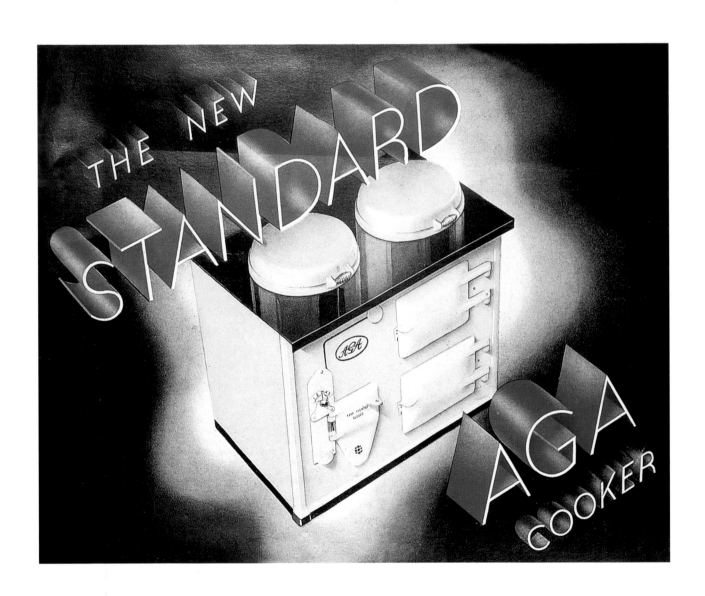

Aga New Standard Stove

Gustav Dalen

Although originally produced by a Swedish company, the Aga has become one of the most enduring and popular symbols of 20th-century British domesticity. The Aga stove combined the traditional range and the cooker, and it was economic, clean, and much admired by professional cooks. The Aga's success, however, rests not so much on these intrinsic qualities as on its capacity to evoke a sense of tradition and domesticity even in the heart of the city.

Physicist Gustav Dalen, who had won the Nobel Prize for physics in 1912, originally designed the Aga in 1922. While president of an acetylene company, Aktiebolaget Gasaccumulator (Amalgamated Gas Accumulator, or AGA), he was temporarily blinded in an experiment. During his convalescence, he noticed that his wife was having problems cooking on a stove. Dalen saw the traditional kitchen range as an outdated relic of the previous century and sought a more reliable and efficient alternative.

The first Aga cooker was licensed for production in Britain in 1929. Made of enameled cast iron and chromium alloy, the Aga is designed to conserve energy and maximize efficiency. It is always ready for cooking since it burns fuel constantly, and the heavily insulated furnace maintains separate, preset temperatures for the different cooking areas. At the same time, the Aga has a low fuel consumption, releasing only enough energy to maintain a comfortable temperature in the surrounding area.

In 1941, under license to AGA, Aga Heat Limited released a range with standardized parts called the Model C, which stayed in production until 1972. Sweden stopped manufacturing Aga cookers when electric stoves came on the market in the 1950s, but in Britain they are still produced by Aga-Rayburn. The fundamental design has changed little in 80 years, although today the Aga can run on gas, oil, or electricity, and not just the traditional solid fuel. In recent years a number of new colors have also been introduced in addition to the original cream.

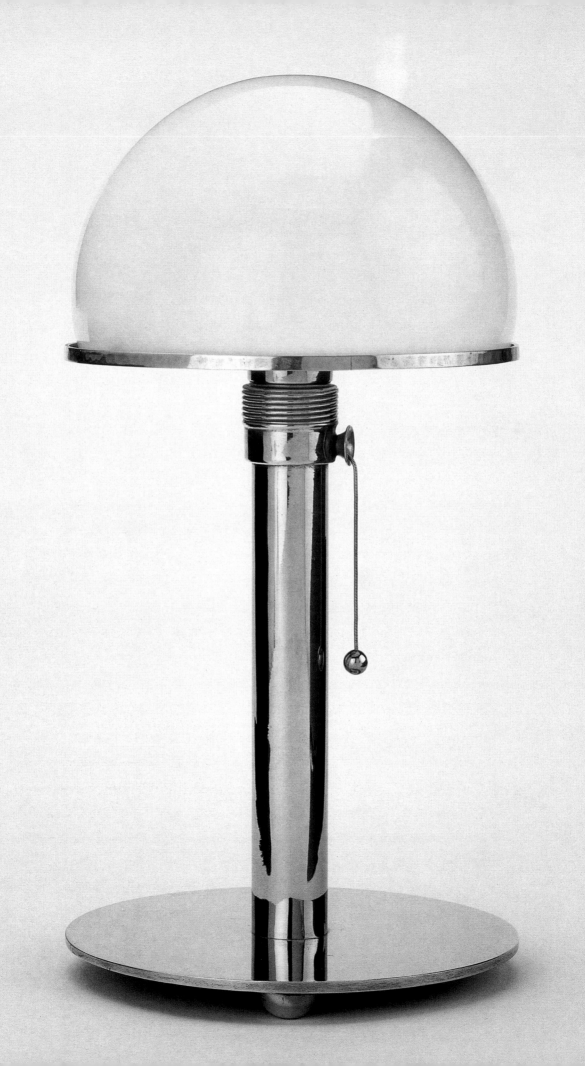

Montblanc Meisterstuck Pen

Montblanc

The Montblanc Meisterstuck pen was not a technological breakthrough, but the strength of its marketing has established it as *the* prestige fountain pen. The German pen manufacturer Montblanc has been making writing instruments since 1910, and its products range from sleek ballpoints to weighty fountain pens. The company sought to position all of its products at the quality end of the market, but only the Meisterstuck survives as a cult object.

The Meisterstuck was designed as a pen that made a strong statement about the owner's taste and social standing. A luxury status symbol that was built to last, it was the first fountain pen to come with a lifetime guarantee. This pen did not mark any radical departure from those already produced by Montblanc—like the other products, it was designed to reflect the ethos of a long tradition of craftsmanship and attention to detail. Although the first Meisterstuck was expensive, it was not so costly as to be the preserve of specialist collectors. It quickly became a bestseller.

The name "Meisterstuck," meaning "masterpiece," is carved emphatically in the gold band around the pen and testifies to the manufacturer's sense of the object's importance. But this is more than mere marketing: the Meisterstuck was recognized as a superior writing tool and is still regarded as such. It is bulky without being cumbersome, its fine balance allowing it to sit comfortably in the hand. Although it was designed in an era of rapid technological advancement, it was intended to evoke nostalgia for days gone by, when luxury items were simple and hand-crafted to perfection. Its simple styling—black plastic with gold trim—professes understated class, but closer inspection reveals a great attention to detail. The white star at the top of the cap suggests the peak of the mountain Mont Blanc, and the figure 4810 inscribed on the nib reminds us of the peak's height in meters. In the modern computer age, this icon of simple penmanship continues to grow in popularity.

Leica Camera

Oskar Barnack

The Leica camera, born from the simple desire to make photography a less arduous business, brought about a revolution in the medium. The 35mm format that was adopted as the starting point for its design turned out to be the size of the future. But the Leica has become a classic for aesthetic as well as for practical reasons.

Early photography involved hauling around heavy metal plates and other cumbersome equipment. The inconvenience of the whole process inspired Oskar Barnack, an engineer and amateur photographer, to investigate new ways of taking photographs. As early as 1905, he had the idea of reducing the format of negatives and then enlarging the photographs after they had been exposed. Ten years later, as development manager at Leica (LEitz CAmera), Barnack was able to put his theory into practice. World War I interrupted his progress, but in 1925, with the backing of his employer, Ernst Leitz II, the Ur-Leica went into production. It was presented to the public that same year, and was followed in 1931 by the Leica 1.

Barnack had created the world's first 35mm camera, and the first small camera to enjoy success in both popular and professional circles, by adapting an instrument designed for taking exposure samples for cinema film. The Leica 1 was even more compact and could be used with interchangeable lenses. It established the benchmark for professional photography in the 1930s. These models were not only more practical than the enormous plate cameras, but also produced better-quality photographs than the contemporary box Brownies and bellows-focus Kodak cameras.

For all Barnack's technical skill, however, it was the shape of the Leica that confirmed it as a classic of its kind. This was a new form for a camera both in terms of external appearance and simplicity of function. Its rounded silhouette, free from unnecessary ornament, has been identified with the ideals of pure design advanced in this period by Barnack's influential contemporaries at the Bauhaus.

Wassily Chair

Marcel Breuer

Wassily Chair

1925

Marcel Breuer
1902–1981

Hungarian

One of the most famous chairs of the 20th century, the Wassily, or B3, chair is still a modernist icon, more than three-quarters of a century after it was designed. It is reputed to have been inspired by the handlebars of a bicycle Marcel Breuer bought in Germany in 1925. The prototypes were produced with the help of a plumber to do the welding, and gradually evolved into the final shape in which legs, arms, and seat rests appear to be formed from a continuous tube. It was a revolutionary design for a club chair that looks both functional and stylish.

In 1920 Breuer studied in the furniture workshop at the Bauhaus design school. He became head of the furniture workshop in 1925, and was strongly influenced by his fellow tutors, who included the Hungarian artist László Moholy-Nagy and the Russian architect and artist El Lissitzky. The Russian artist Wassily Kandinsky, then also a Bauhaus tutor, gave Breuer's design his approval, and that is how the chair came to be named after him.

The Bauhaus, directed by Walter Gropius, was keen to develop links between design and industry and to blur the distinction between art and craftmaking, so the fact that this chair was produced by Breuer in his own studios outside the Bauhaus, and went directly into manufacture with German furniture company Standard-Möbel, displeased Gropius. However, the use of tubular steel in furniture became one of the strongest design influences of the Bauhaus.

Breuer was unusual in that his career progressed from furniture designer to architect, and his furniture—with its strong structural form and spatial awareness—can be seen as a rehearsal for his later buildings. Breuer and Gropius, both Jewish, left Nazi Germany for England in 1935, and went to the United States two years later, where they worked as architects and teachers. The Wassily chair is still in production, and its style and ingenuity make it an enduring symbol of prestige in offices and showrooms.

BAUHAUSVERLAG

MÜNCHEN
Wormserstraße 1

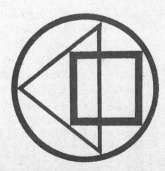

BAUHAUS
BÜCHER

Hanging Lamp

Poul Henningsen

Poul Henningsen's hanging lamp appeared at a time when designs for electric lighting were being radically rethought. Designers wanted to achieve more than simply designing around the bulb—they sought also to provide different qualities of light. Henningsen's achievement was his innovation in the design of the shade, which gave direct and indirect light without glare. In 1926 this was a new lighting concept. Henningsen's lights became universally popular features of the modernist interior, and were, for example, used by German architect Ludwig Mies van der Rohe in his famous 1929 Tugendhat House in Brno (now in the Czech Republic). The lamp remains a classic modernist object.

Henningsen trained as an architect in Copenhagen, designing theaters, restaurants, and houses that established his international reputation. He was also known as a writer and journalist. In the late 1920s, he edited a journal with Danish architect and designer Kaare Klint called *Kritisk Revy*, which was the most influential architectural magazine in Denmark. It proclaimed the importance of standards in design and sought to make artists and designers aware of and responsive to the 20th century. Henningsen maintained that it was necessary to blur the distinction between art and design, and emphasized the importance of functionalism: "make things which are fit for use!"

In 1926 he was awarded the contract to design lighting for the Forum, which was a large exhibition hall in Copenhagen then under construction. Based on the original hanging lamp design, the fittings that he produced for this were manufactured by Danish firm Louis Poulsen, and went into mass-production as the PH series. Henningsen's lamps were created for different purposes and places, and were given specific tonalities with the use of different-colored metals for the three or more diffusing saucers. In the 21st century, his lamps and the imitations they inspired continue to have appeal for both domestic and business use.

c. 1926

Lalique Oranges Vase

René Lalique

Lalique Oranges Vase

c. 1926

René Lalique
1860–1945

French

The work of René Lalique represents the continuing French tradition of high-quality decorative glass. Starting his career as a jeweler, Lalique's success began with his exhibits at the Paris Exposition Universelle et Internationale of 1900. He went on to establish a distinguished clientele, including the French actress Sarah Bernhardt.

By 1890 Lalique had already opened an experimental glass furnace and was exploring different glass techniques, and after 1902 he opened various studios to produce glass and other work in ivory, enamel, and alabaster. After 1906 he worked with the French parfumier François Coty to make perfume bottles, and opened factories at various locations outside Paris. Gradually, his work in glass came to dominate, and by 1914 he concentrated his efforts entirely in this medium.

In 1925 the Exposition des Arts Décoratifs et Industriels Modernes in Paris, from which the "Art Deco" style gets its name, was staged. It was devoted mainly to French work, and contained elaborately-staged room settings with furniture by designers such as Jacques-Emile Ruhlmann and Jean Dunand. Lalique exhibited here too, displaying many different glass objects, such as vases, bowls, and candlesticks. The exhibitition proved to be the highlight of Lalique's career as a *verrier*, or "glass artist." His fame spread rapidly—his designs were perfectly attuned to the times, and he was shrewd enough to mass-produce objects that were regarded as works of great luxury.

Lalique's adventurous techniques allowed him to produce many different effects that incorporated three-dimensional ornament—such as classical motifs, animals, and plants—and which combined opalescent, frosted, colored, and polished glass. His molds were used for blown, molten, and pressed glass, and the prototypes were gradually adapted, reused, and replaced. The vase shown here is a classic Lalique Art Deco piece, both in its shape and its raised, stylized decoration in enameled glass, in sober tones of pale green and dark gray.

Rolex Oyster Perpetual Watch

Rolex

The Rolex Oyster Perpetual watch has become inextricably linked with luxury and wealth. So strong are these associations that ownership of the watch sends out a strong signal of ambition, social positioning, and aspirations to success. The Rolex was invented in 1926 as the first truly waterproof watch, and tested successfully during a cross-English-Channel swim in 1927. Rolex continued its technical innovations in 1931 with the introduction of the Rolex Perpetual, which had the advantage of being the first self-winding watch. Since then many other models have been developed with different mechanisms to suit extreme conditions, as well as new styling and features—the Day-Date Oyster watch, for example, displays the days of the week in a choice of 26 languages. The model shown here is an Oyster Perpetual Date men's watch. It was made in 1965 and has the distinctive bracelet that typifies the brand.

The Rolex Oyster is the epitome of precise Swiss workmanship with no expense spared in the quality of the parts. The cases are made of solid stainless steel, gold, or platinum with a unique serial number. The crystal is cut from a block of synthetic sapphire, its Cyclops lens magnifies the date two and half times to make it easily visible, and the winding crown is twinlock or triplock, giving maximum protection against dust and water. Each watch is tested by the Swiss Chronometers Control Office for 15 days continuously before receiving a red seal and the inscription "superlative chronometer officially certified."

This legendary Swiss technology does not, however, entirely explain the cult status of the Rolex Oyster. In the period after World War II, that status is more likely due to the celebrities who wore the watch, notably Ian Fleming's fictional hero James Bond. The enduring popularity of the Rolex can also be seen in world-renowned auction rooms, such as Sotheby's in London, where the earlier models often fetch higher prices than the contemporary models.

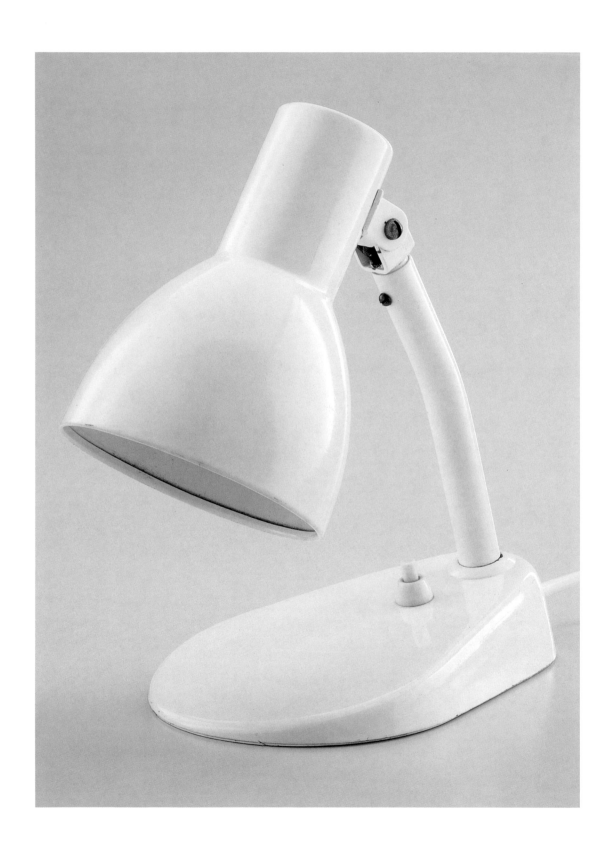

1928

Kandem Lamp

Marianne Brandt

Kandem Lamp

1928

Marianne Brandt
1893–1983

German

Marianne Brandt was not only one of the first women to design in metal at the Bauhaus design school, but was also one of very few female industrial designers of the 20th century. One important strategy for the Bauhaus was developing partnerships with industry, and this flexible metal bedside lamp was one of the first Bauhaus-designed products to go into mass-production. Its simple, radical design helped to establish lighting as a product category in its own right, and it has influenced the design of downlighter lamps ever since.

Brandt started out as a painter and joined the Bauhaus in 1924, where she worked in the metal workshop, which was then run by the Hungarian artist László Moholy-Nagy. The founder of the Bauhaus, Walter Gropius, had attracted such distinguished artists as Russians Wassily Kandinsky and El Lissitzky, and the Swiss painter Paul Klee, as well as Moholy-Nagy. Gropius intended to strike a balance between the process of production, led by workshop masters, and the process of designing, led by artist form masters. This strategy offered Brandt the opportunity to develop into one of the Bauhaus's most prolific designers, and she had an adventurous eye for spotting the potentials of the various metals in the studio. She served as assistant master of the metal workshop until 1928, and for a short time as head, before leaving to work in Gropius's architectural office in Berlin in 1929.

The Kandem lamp was designed as a class project, and was produced in nickel-plated metal and lacquered. Simple in construction and practical to use, it has a push-button switch that is easy to find in the dark. Using few component parts, the base and stand are ingeniously shaped and balanced to be stylish, stable, and yet simple to manufacture. It was first produced by German firm Körting & Mathiesen in Leipzig, and 50,000 were sold between 1928 and 1932. Brandt later designed for the Ruppelwerk metalwork factory in Gotha, Germany, and taught in Dresden and Berlin.

Chaise Longue B306

Charlotte Perriand, Le Corbusier, and Pierre Jeanneret

Chaise Longue

1928–1929

Charlotte Perriand
1903–1999
Le Corbusier 1887–1965
Pierre Jeanneret
1896–1967

Swiss/French

In the 1920s Swiss-French architect Charles-Édouard Janneret, better known as Le Corbusier, started to design radical new buildings in France, such as the Villa Stein at Garches and the Villa Savoye outside Paris, which he called "machines for living." These geometric houses offered original and new open-plan spatial divisions with different levels at the front and back. The modernist spaces within them needed furniture, and at first Le Corbusier looked at existing pieces that may have been suitable—for example, chairs manufactured by the Austrian firm Thonet or leather seats traditionally used in English gentlemen's clubs. It was inevitable, however, that he would look to designing radical new furniture to suit his vision for 20th-century living.

Le Corbusier set up a division to design furniture in his architectural practice in Paris, and invited a young unknown architect, Charlotte Perriand, to join his team in 1927. Perriand experimented with tubular steel and natural materials, and had exhibited her "Roof bar," a radically minimalist glass and metal space, earlier that year.

While the concept was Le Corbusier's, the execution and design of this chair is now recognized as belonging principally to Perriand. The chair is placed on an H-shaped steel support, with the curved tubular-steel frame supporting the stretched cowhide, allowing for a full-length lounging position with both head and foot support. The juxtaposition of the "engineer aesthetic" of the frame and the relaxed body shape of the lounger produced a "confrontation" that interested and occupied Perriand.

Le Corbusier, his architect cousin Pierre Jeanneret, and Perriand exhibited this chaise longue at the Salon d'Automne in Paris in 1929. It was initially produced by Thonet, and was later reproduced in 1965 and in the 1980s by Italian firm Cassina. For all its rational and modernist design, this chair is purely for leisure, and its different positions encourage the most relaxed poses. More importantly, however, it gives a sculptural presence to the spacious and light interior of many modern homes.

Barcelona Chair

Ludwig Mies van der Rohe

Barcelona Chair

1929

Ludwig Mies van der Rohe
1886–1969

German

The Barcelona chair was designed for the German Pavilion at the 1929 Exposición Internacional de Barcelona, in Spain. The pavilion was a landmark in the architectural modern movement—it was a one-story building with marble and onyx walls, tinted, semireflecting glass, and sharp-edged stainless steel and travertine (a type of limestone). Demolished at the end of the exhibition, it has since been reconstructed as an architectural icon, complete with furniture, as seen here.

The chair was one of two, together with footstools and table, that Ludwig Mies van der Rohe designed as a modern throne for the King and Queen of Spain when they opened the Exposición. Designed with the assistance of Lilly Reich, a student at the Bauhaus design school in Germany, it has an X-frame made of two flat steel bars on each side that were originally chrome-plated steel but became stainless steel. One bar runs in a single curve from the back to the front leg, and the other has two curves and supports the seat and back leg. This neat shape, with its regal overtones that allude to the X-shape used on a medieval royal chair, legitimized the use of metal for luxury furniture. The original upholstery was white, black, or tan tufted leather.

At this time Mies van der Rohe was practicing as an architect and designer in Germany. He designed his own house and other private houses for which he always designed the furniture and fittings too. He was director of the Bauhaus for its last three years, and in 1938 left for the United States. There he became a leading exponent of the International Style, producing elegant skyscrapers—such as the Seagram Building in New York (1954–1958)—with pared-down shapes built from luxurious materials.

Though never intended for mass-production, the Barcelona chair was widely produced, mostly by hand, in Europe. After World War II it was revived, slightly modified, by American furniture manufacturer Knoll International. It continues to be an imposing piece, lending stylish modernity to the lobbies of large multinationals.

Bialetti Moka Express Coffee Maker

Alfonso Bialetti

The angular, hexagonal shape of the Bialetti Moka Express coffee maker, with its aluminum body and Bakelite knob and handle, belong to the Art Deco period in which it was invented. The Moka Express is, however, more than a period design—its stylish and functional aesthetic has come to represent Italian national identity in design.

Its inventor, Alfonso Bialetti, had learned the technique of aluminum manufacture in Paris in 1933, when he worked with the chilling, turning, and finishing phases of boilers. Until 1939, the Moka Express coffee maker was made manually, and more than 70,000 machines were produced by this method. After World War II, production was organized on an industrial scale, and this hitherto unpatented machine was given patented technical specifications. A logo was designed, based on a cartoon by Renato Bialetti, Alfonso's son, which appears on every Moka coffee maker, and the new, low-cost Bialetti machine was launched on the market. The product has continued to maintain its lead and still produces two-thirds of the espresso coffee in Italian homes.

The Moka Express was designed as a stove-top coffee maker for the home, and one of its attractions is that it is simple to use, sturdy, and incorporates no complicated machinery. Water and steam from the bottom compartment pass through the middle, which is filled with finely ground beans, to fill the top section with freshly made coffee. It is well balanced with a level handle and spout that makes pouring accurate and safe, and it conveniently makes small amounts of strong espresso coffee.

The design of the Moka Express has been copied by several Italian coffee makers. In the 1970s German designer Richard Sapper imitated it with a more complicated and expensive machine for Italian design company Alessi. In 1984 it was revived by the Italian architect Aldo Rossi, who produced a version, again for Alessi, that retained the hexagonal shape and the level spout and handle, although Rossi's version had straight sides in a taller, slimmer model with a higher lid.

London Underground Map

Henry C. Beck

London Underground Map

1933

Henry C. Beck
1903–1974

British

This diagrammatic map of the London Underground (subway) system was a landmark in the representation of public transport information, and has remained a classic in graphic design. It flouted the traditional map-making precedents in two ways: it distorted the proportion of the central area, enlarging it so that the complex connections could be made clear; and it limited the direction of route lines to vertical, horizontal, and diagonal, which was a schematic plan more akin to an electrical circuit.

Between the world wars, London Transport (LT) became a pioneer of modern design, led by the vision of one man, Frank Pick. Pick joined London Underground in 1906, and in 1916 commissioned British calligrapher and type-designer Edward Johnston to design Railway, a modern sans-serif type, and a bull's-eye symbol, still in use today, that established a corporate identity for LT. When Pick became vice-chairman and chief executive of the London Passenger Board in the 1930s, he extended his vision, commissioning artists of international standing to design posters for the Underground, such as the American Edward McKnight Kauffer and Britons Edward Bawden and Graham Sutherland.

Henry C. Beck was an electrical draftsman with London Transport, and his map arose from a sketch in a school textbook that he did in 1931. Pick recognized its originality, and it was given a first trial printing in 1933. Once the map was published, far left, its concise clarity made it easy for the public to follow, and it became extremely popular, facilitating travel on what rapidly became the world's most complex subway system. Beck became a freelance draftsman but continued his work on the map over the next two decades, modifying it and adapting it until 1959. With modifications, it still reflects his original vision, and remains functional and contemporary 70 years after it was first designed.

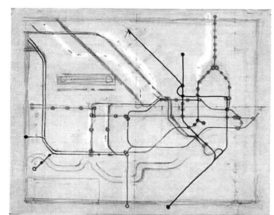

As his sketch shows, Beck's masterstroke was to depict the subway routes as if they were electrical circuits.

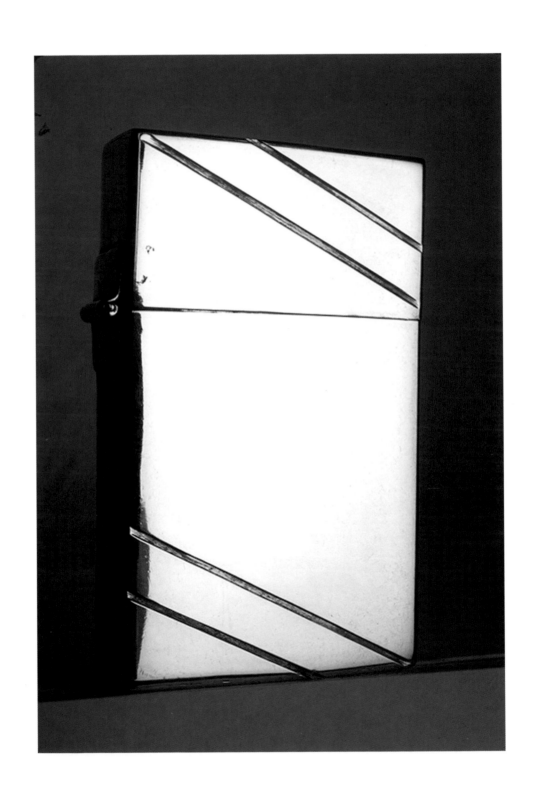

Zippo Lighter

George G. Blaisdell

Zippo Lighter

1933

George G. Blaisdell
1895–1978

American

The Zippo lighter represents a certain kind of American male "cool"—there are countless cigarette lighters, but there is only one Zippo. What was designed with utility in mind quickly became a collector's item and a statement of effortless style. More than 325 million windproof Zippo lighters have been produced since 1933.

American businessman George G. Blaisdell, reputedly not himself a cigarette smoker, founded Zippo in Bradford, Pennsylvania, in 1933 with the intention of creating a cheap (the original price was $1.95) and easy-to-use cigarette lighter. He obtained the rights to an Austrian windproof lighter with a removable top and redesigned it to his own requirements. He made the case rectangular, attached the lid with a welded hinge, and surrounded the wick with a windshield. His fascination with another recent invention, the zipper, gave rise to the name. Backed with a lifetime guarantee, the product was an instant success and made Blaisdell a fortune. The company is still owned by second- and third-generation members of his family.

Apart from improvements in the flint wheel and modifications in case finishes, Blaisdell's original design—with burnished steel body, fliptop cover, and rolling flint—remains virtually unchanged after 70 years. Zippos are made only at Bradford and Niagara Falls, Ontario, and the location is stamped on the base of each one. The Zippo guarantee still promises: "It works or we fix it free," and the company's confidence is borne out by stories such as the one about the lighter that was removed from the belly of a fish and lit first time. The brand has expanded to include products such as pocket knives and writing instruments, but Zippo's reputation still rests in its original lighter.

George G. Blaisdell, above, with a promotional model of his famous cigarette lighter.

Coldspot Super Six Refrigerator

Raymond Loewy

Raymond Loewy remains one of the best-known designers of the 20th century. It was Loewy, with a group of his contemporaries, who helped create the profession of industrial design in the 1920s and 1930s, and focused on design as a way to increase consumer sales. He trained as an engineer in France, where he received his degree in 1918, and emigrated to the United States in 1919. There he freelanced in various design jobs, before setting up his industrial design firm in 1929.

At that time the science of streamlining was advancing rapidly. It was made possible by new techniques in metal stamping that allowed for the shallow curves that characterized the streamlined look in automobiles, trains, and domestic appliances. Loewy's aim was to capture the imagination of the public by producing designs that were modern and exciting. With the Coldspot Super Six, he transformed the domestic fridge into an object of desire, a modernist sculpture for the kitchen—sexy and deeply desirable. Domestic fridges had been available since 1913 in the United States, but the initial models were cumbersome with a bulky mechanism and little storage space. Loewy's refrigerator was an exterior remake of these early appliances, which had been divided into two rectangular panels. His design unified the front with rounded corners and edges, giving it an up-to-date, sculptured look. The door hinges were hidden, the handle responded to a light touch, and a tasteful feature was made of the logo and nameplate. The shelves were made from rustproof aluminum, which was a practical improvement to the interior.

Loewy, pictured near left, designed the Coldspot for the mail-order firm Sears Roebuck, and in 1934 the firm's sales rose 400 percent. This increase was the result not so much of superior engineering but of styling, of which Loewy was an acknowledged and much-admired master. He appeared on the cover of *Time* magazine in 1949, headlined as the man who "streamlines the sales curve."

Ekco AD65 Circular Radio

Wells Coates

Wells Coates was a modernist architect who was born in Tokyo, Japan, but later emigrated to Canada where he trained as an engineer. In 1922 he moved to London, first studying for a PhD in engineering before settling on a career in design and architecture in 1928 after an influential visit to the 1925 Paris Exposition des Arts Décoratifs et Industriels Modernes. One of his first jobs, in 1931, was with the British Raymond McGrath and the Russian Serge Chermayeff, both architect-designers, to design the interiors and studios of the modernist Broadcasting House in London, home of the British Broadcasting Corporation (BBC). This gave Coates a chance to combine his engineering expertise and his new enthusiasm for compact, minimalist design. The studios remain classic examples of modernism in a working environment.

Radios—or wireless sets, as they were known in the 1930s—were prize possessions that cut across class boundaries and were the main and most immediate source of news and entertainment until after World War II and the advent of television. The circular radio was produced after Coates won a competition held in 1932 by Eric Cole, managing director of the manufacturing firm Ekco, to design the ideal plastic radio.

Coates had been attracted by simple forms in his youth in Japan, and was able to combine this influence with the pared-down style of the post-Bauhaus period in his radio design. The shape of the circular speaker was echoed by the semicircular tuning dial, which gave the user the illusion that they were searching the world for stations. The control buttons complete the circle around the speaker. The compact design reduced tooling costs and facilitated production—a later, cheaper version had a walnut look—and the case, molded in the new Bakelite material, gave the radio a rather technical look and distinguished it from the previous models that had been set in wooden cabinets and looked like furniture. The AD65 was produced by Ekco, with variations, from 1934 until 1946.

Kit Kat Chocolate Bar

Rowntrees

Kit Kat, a chocolate wafer cookie, is now an international brand and one of the world's best-known snacks. It was originally launched in Britain in September 1935 as Chocolate Crisp, and allegedly took its later, more catchy title from the Kit Kat Club, an 18th-century literary club for the British aristocracy. The club's low-ceilinged rooms could only accommodate long, narrow, strip-like paintings—known as "kit kats" in the art world—so it is possible that the brand name drew its inspiration from these.

Double-wrapped in foil with a distinctive red-and-white outer wrapper made of paper, Kit Kat was an immediate success. Part of the bar's obvious appeal was that it came in four breakable sections, which could be shared with others. Kit Kat quickly became the leading brand for one of Britain's best-known chocolate companies, Rowntrees. A Quaker confectionery company in York, England, Rowntrees was founded in 1862 under the name Rowntree Cocoa Works, and provided employment, a school, and health facilities for a large number of employees.

Kit Kat's success is due not only to its combination of ingredients, but also to its distinctive logo, packaging, and marketing. It was an early product to be advertised on British television, first appearing in 1957. Its catchphrase, "Have a break, have a Kit Kat"—referring both to commercial breaks in TV programs and to the snap of the bars—proved to be one of the enduring slogans for an entire generation. When milk shortages at the end of World War II made it necessary for the bar to be covered in dark, rather than milk, chocolate, the bar's original red-and-white packaging was changed to blue and white for two years to indictate the temporary change.

In 1988, Rowntrees was taken over by the Swiss confectionery company Nestlé, who continue to develop the brand. Since then, Nestlé has replaced the foil and paper covering with a single plastic wrapper, to the dismay of many consumers. In 1999 it also introduced a "chunky" version, but this has not supplanted the standard product.

Red Telephone Box

Sir Giles Gilbert Scott

Red Telephone Box

1935

Sir Giles Gilbert Scott
1880–1960

British

The red telephone box (booth) remains one of the most instantly recognizable emblems of British national identity. When production stopped in the 1960s, the modern replacements were universally attacked as bland and lacking in character.

In 1924 the public telephone network in Britain—the General Post Office (GPO)—organized a national competition for a new telephone booth. Sir Giles Gilbert Scott submitted his design and won the high-profile competition. He was, in many ways, a surprising choice of designer—as an architect, his masterpiece was Liverpool Cathedral in England, an imposing but hardly inspirational building. However, by approaching the telephone box in purely architectural terms, Scott's achievement was to make an essentially functional object a hugely popular piece of street furniture. Scott took his inspiration from the works of the architect Sir John Soane, whom he championed.

Scott originally thought that silver might best complement his design, but the GPO, knowing what would best stand out, preferred red. The red telephone box is properly called the K6, or Jubilee Kiosk, and was produced to commemorate the silver jubilee of King George V in 1935. The K1, Scott's first attempt at a standardized kiosk, underwent a series of modifications that culminated in the K6, and a few examples of this classic design can still be seen today. It retained the distinctive domed roof of the original, had more modern glazing, the crown was embossed rather than pierced, and the interior details were upgraded with the addition of an umbrella hook and mirror.

Scott's design was not universally admired—modernists regretted its reliance on traditional architectural thinking; conservatives thought it brash and incongruous, especially when sited in rural areas. However, Scott's kiosk overcame initial resistance to become an internationally recognized symbol of Britain. His achievement was to convey dignity, sturdiness, and a sense of security, while housing a piece of technology that was transforming communication in an unprecedented fashion.

Ballpoint Pen

László Biró

Ballpoint Pen

1938

László Biró
1899–1985

Hungarian

Until the early 20th century it was a 19th-century invention—the fountain pen—that was popularly used by people when writing in ink. In the 20th century, however, people wanted an ink equivalent to the pencil that did not require refilling and was disposable, clean, and easy to use. Although there had been a "ballpoint" pen invented as early as 1888 by an American, J. J. Loud, which was used for marking leather, the wider applications were not recognized, and many technical problems remained unresolved.

The story of the development of ballpoint pens as an essential 20th-century tool is a complicated one of patents, innovations, and marketing. László József Biró was the true pioneer of today's ballpoint pen. A journalist, he experimented with a quick-drying printing ink that did not smudge. As this ink was too thick to be used in a fountain pen, Biró devised a ballpoint mechanism, and in 1942 his brother, Georg, a chemist, invented a special ink that flowed more satisfactorily.

After World War II, an English accountant called Henry George Martin, who had invested in Biró's company, brought the patented pens back to England under license. He sold them to the Royal Air Force (RAF) and the American forces, where they were taken up in great numbers as they were leakproof even in unpressurized aircraft. At first these ballpoints were very costly and were sold to the public only as expensive prestige items. However, in 1949 Italian-born French businessman Marcel Bich came up with a plastic version that was much cheaper and was a runaway sales success. In 1957 his company Société BIC bought up Biró Swan, which was a descendant of Martin's company, and the BIC Biro, which is now thought of as *the* biro, was launched.

The BIC "Crystal" pen is its most popular descendant, particularly the version with the clear plastic barrel that shows how much ink remains. Over the years, the problems with blotching and smudging have been largely eliminated, and there are versions of the pen in four different colors—red, green, blue, and black.

Gaggia Espresso Machine

Achille Gaggia

Gaggia Espresso Machine

1938

Achille Gaggia
1895–1961

Italian

The ritual of making, serving, and consuming coffee has come to represent Italian style and culture. After World War II—when all things Italian were imitated all over the world—Italian coffee bars seemed to offer access to a glamorous world. The image of Italy as romantic and chic was promoted by such Hollywood films as *Roman Holiday* (1953), and the Italian Vespa scooter epitomized a stylish, youthful mode of transport.

The first espresso machine had been patented in Italy in 1902 by Luigi Besseraand. The original Italian invention was inspired by the desire to speed up the brewing process and produce a strong, individual cup of coffee. These first machines were steam-driven and required considerable skill in controlling the heat source, the steam pressure, and the hot water valve. The process was not popularized, however, until bartender Achille Gaggia designed his domestic machine in the late 1930s—and the first models would not be produced until 1948, after the end of the war.

Gaggia had grown dissatisfied with the traditional coffee machines he was operating. He experimented with several prototypes, including the patent to use steam pressure to heat and froth milk. He went on to develop his spring-piston machine that produced a higher and more exact pressure on the coffee grounds. Later machines used electric pumps to supply constant pressure, and heat exchangers to keep the water below boiling point. The craze for cappuccino coffee had begun.

Gaggia's glamorous-looking coffee machine changed the whole coffee-drinking scene. Coffee shops opened with machines that made the famous whooshing noise and produced both small, inky black drinks or large, frothy confections served in characteristic Italian cups. The shops, with names such as El Cubano, became part of the urban way of life, and young people found a smart, informal meeting place that did not restrict the time at the table or result in a hefty check for food. The gleaming machines behind the counter also added just the right ingredient of style.

Kubus Glassware

Wilhelm Wagenfeld

Kubus Glassware

1938

Wilhelm Wagenfeld
1900–1990

German

The new inventions of the 20th century required new designs to complement them, that were both functional and in keeping with contemporary aesthetics. The development of the electric refrigerator brought with it the need for practical, hygienic storage containers, and glass was the obvious material to use. There already existed stacking glassware for refrigerators that were made in the United States, but Wagenfeld's design was the first in Germany. This set of refrigerator containers is an example of the close contact he had with that country's glass-manufacturing industry.

Wilhelm Wagenfeld trained at the German design school the Bauhaus, which he joined in 1923. While there, he worked with German glassware company Jenaer Glaswerke Schott & Genossen, where he combined the techniques of blown glass with pressed glass. In 1935, as the result of a lecture he gave which greatly impressed Dr. Karl Mey, chairman of Vereingte Lausitzer Glaswerke (VLG), a German glassware manufacturer, Wagenfeld was appointed artistic director of the company.

During the late 1930s, Wagenfeld's designs became more industrial in appearance. With these containers that were mass-produced by VLG, he further developed his ideas using pressed glass, and his design is a continuation of the simple shapes he had seen at the Bauhaus. The sizes are carefully standardized and adjusted to one another to occupy minimum space. The handles and lips are ingeniously set into the corners of the pouring vessels so that the stacking symmetry and the geometric whole are not disturbed. The containers use interchangeable lids of different sizes, some with pouring lips and handles, and all with air vents. The idea of combining square containers rather than attempting to squash together traditional round storage jars is still a practical solution, and the jars continue to be produced exactly as they were designed in 1938. Wagenfeld stressed the social responsibility played by design, and these inexpensive, functional containers for ordinary people exemplify that vision.

Volkswagen Beetle

Ferdinand Porsche and Erwin Komenda

Volkswagen Beetle

1938

Ferdinand Porsche
1875–1951
Erwin Komenda
1904–1966

German

Although a new model was launched in 1998, the classic Beetle, right, has remained relatively unchanged since 1938.

In 1972 the Volkswagen Beetle superceded Ford's Model T as the most produced car in history. Ferdinand Porsche, a one-time electrical engineer and designer of the Mercedes SS sports car, had long wanted to build a modern, European equivalent of the Ford Model T. In the 1930s, with the support of Adolf Hitler, who shared his vision of a Germany where every citizen could own a car, Porsche began work on the design of Hitler's so-called *Kraft durch Freude* car ("strength through joy"), or KdF-Wagen—a design that would change little throughout the Beetle's long history. Sparing no expense, he chose a costly, air-cooled, horizontally opposed engine because of its full-throttle endurance and took the unprecedented step of placing the engine at the back of the car. Porsche concentrated on the technical side, but the distinctive body shape was conceived by the German aerodynamics expert Erwin Komenda. On seeing it in 1938, the *New York Times* derisively dubbed the new car the "Beetle." Early models were later improved with the addition of bumpers and running boards.

Properly known as the Volkswagen ("people's car"), the vehicle was exhibited publicly in 1939 and sold through an impractical payment scheme. It was only after World War II, however, that Hitler's supposed dream became a reality. In 1945 the Volkswagen factory at Wolfsburg, which had manufactured armaments during the war, came under British administration. In 1946 the British authorities ordered 20,000 cars from the factory, and the Volkswagen became a symbol of Germany's reconstruction. Crucially, however, America remained skeptical, and it was not until the 1960s, on the back of one of the most successful advertising campaigns ever, that it achieved international popularity—at its peak in 1968, 430,000 were sold in the United States.

Citroën 2CV

Pierre Boulanger

Citroën 2CV

1939

Pierre Boulanger
1886–1950

France

The Citroën 2CV became the most successful French car ever, and still has a unique place in the affections of the French public. Its image was that of a vehicle that was cheap, cheerful, and easy to maintain, yet at the same time quirky and stylish.

Frenchman André-Gustave Citroën started manufacturing car components in 1905, but had to turn to ordnance for the French Army in 1913. After World War I, he reconverted his factory and returned to the production of small, inexpensive vehicles. Citroën first hired Jules Saloman as his designer, and they produced innovative models for the mass market, including the very successful 5CV. Then Citroën, whose ideas were often ahead of his time, overinvested in the company, which was taken over by French tire manufacturer Michelin in 1934, with the name and reputation retained.

The 2CV, designed by Pierre Boulanger, first appeared in 1939, but World War II halted production. It was finally launched in 1948 to rival the Volkswagen Beetle and the Renault 4CV as the "people's car"—one that was inexpensive to build and maintain. Boulanger is quoted as saying he wanted "an umbrella on four wheels." His design was known as the Deux Chevaux ("two horses"), and although it had a low horsepower, the engine was air-cooled and the pressed-metal body was technologically advanced, though still within the car's low budget.

Originally, left, the 2CV had one headlamp and a single windscreen wiper—which were later standardized as pairs—but its gate-opening doors and windows with folding glass flaps, instead of wind-down windows, persisted. The priority was maximizing the space inside: seats folded down to accommodate long, awkward objects, the retractable roof allowed tall pieces to be carried, and the excellent suspension withstood heavy weights on country roads at a time when France was largely rural. As with many meticulously designed functional objects, eventually the 2CV was more than simply a utilitarian vehicle and became a smart, desirable car for city dwellers.

Tupperware

Earl S. Tupper

Tupperware

1946

Earl S. Tupper
1907–1983

American

Tupperware parties, left and far right, allowed women to see the latest products in the privacy of their homes.

Tupperware is a 20th-century success story involving a new material, clever design, and marketing skill. Earl S. Tupper founded the Tupper Plastics Company in 1938, setting up his first factory in 1942 and producing the original household wares in 1946. The business was not a success until 1951, when sales representative Brownie Wise came up with one of the legendary marketing concepts of the 20th century—Tupperware parties. Here, women were able to meet socially and to buy goods from a Tupperware representative. A complete range of items was displayed and the "guests" were persuaded to purchase a good selection, with the promise that the goods demonstrably worked and were made from polyethylene, which was designed to last a lifetime.

Most plastics at that time were duroplastics, such as Bakelite, and could not withstand heat. Tupper's breakthrough was to use thermoplastic polyethylene, which remains soft and moldable when subjected to heat. The products had air-tight seals to keep food fresh, and prevent it from picking

Enjoy A Popular TUPPERWARE Private Showing

Private Showings Are Fun ...Morning, Afternoon Or Evening!

up other odors from the refrigerator. The method of closing the containers had to be observed exactly—the lid had to be fitted down before lifting the corner to expel any air—and was demonstrated at the parties.

The Tupperware range included containers to store a wide variety of goods, such as cookies, cakes, cheese, and even salads. In addition to storage for dry foods, there was tableware, picnic mugs for children, and jugs for drinks with lids that were reliably leak-proof—unique at that time. A good color range also made it tempting to build up sets. In 1990 the range was redesigned by Morrison Cousins, vice-president of design for the Tupperware Corporation, and many other items have since been added.

Vespa Motor Scooter

Corradino d'Ascanio

Vespa Motor Scooter

1946

Corradino d'Ascanio
1891–1981

Italian

Just as German designer Ferdinand Porsche designed a "car for the people"—the Volkswagen Beetle—Corradino d'Ascanio's design was a "scooter for the people." The Vespa was simple to use, economical, and aesthetically pleasing. This utililty vehicle captured the collective imagination and became not just a symbol of postwar Italy—a metaphor for reconstruction—but an internationally recognized icon.

The Italian Piaggio Company, which continues to produce Vespas, was founded in Genoa in 1884 by Rinaldo Piaggio. After his death in 1938, the business was passed on to his two sons, Enrico and Armando. Piaggio produced fighter aircraft throughout both World Wars, but Enrico Piaggio was quick to realize that he would have to find a new product for his company in peacetime. As Italy struggled to rebuild, gasoline and automobiles were in short supply and very expensive—most Italians had turned to bicycles for transportation. Piaggio, his factory almost completely destroyed, had come across a scooter used by paratroopers during the war. He saw it as a solution both to the country's transportation problem and to his own need to continue production.

Piaggio's first attempt at building a scooter was in 1945. It was called Paperino (Donald Duck), and its odd appearance was ridiculed by the press. Undeterred, he enlisted Corradino d'Ascanio, an aeronautical engineer. D'Ascanio adopted "stress-skin" technology, which treats body and frame as a single entity and which owes much to the visual vocabulary of American streamlining. The concealment of the engine beneath sheet metal marked the biggest departure from traditional motorcycle construction, and the step-through design made the scooter easy for both men and women to use. It is said that when Piaggio first heard it run, he remarked that it reminded him of a wasp—a *vespa*, in Italian, hence its name. D'Ascanio's design had its debut at the 1946 Turin Show, and over 100 models have since been produced. A new generation of the Vespa was launched in 1996, on the scooter's 50th anniversary.

Wurlitzer Jukebox 1015

Paul Fuller

Wurlitzer Jukebox 1015

1946–1947

Paul Fuller
1897–1951

American

The Wurlitzer family had been buying and selling musical instruments in Saxony, Germany, as far back as 1659. Rudolph Wurlitzer moved to the United States in 1853, founded the Rudolph Wurlitzer Company in 1856, and became the largest instrument supplier in the country. The first Wurlitzer coin-operated electric piano was built in 1896, and with the advent of movies, the company became synonymous with the large organs that accompanied silent films. In the early 1930s the Depression almost finished Wurlitzer, but the end of Prohibition in 1933 saw a renewed demand for coin-operated music, and the company launched its first jukebox, named the Debutante. Little is known about Paul Fuller, but his 1938 design, Model 24, was the first in a series of machines that gave Wurlitzer market dominance for the next 10 years. As a result, Wurlitzer took the unprecedented step of crediting him with the design—most jukebox designers remain anonymous. It was not until 1946, however, that Fuller created what has become the classic jukebox—the Wurlitzer 1015.

The 1015 combined the best elements from earlier models (changing colors, bubble tubes, and ornate metalwork) and presented them in a streamlined package. In design terms, however, it was not especially innovative, and its success was primarily due to Wurlitzer's marketing. Jukebox advertising had previously targeted potential owners who would see these machines as a financial investment to attract customers. Wurlitzer mythologized its new product, placing it as a cornerstone of idealized family life, and then sold this idea direct to the public. The nostalgic images that popularized "America's favorite nickel's worth of fun" underlie the jukebox's continuing iconic status.

Clever marketing, above, elevated the Wurlitzer jukebox to the status of cultural icon.

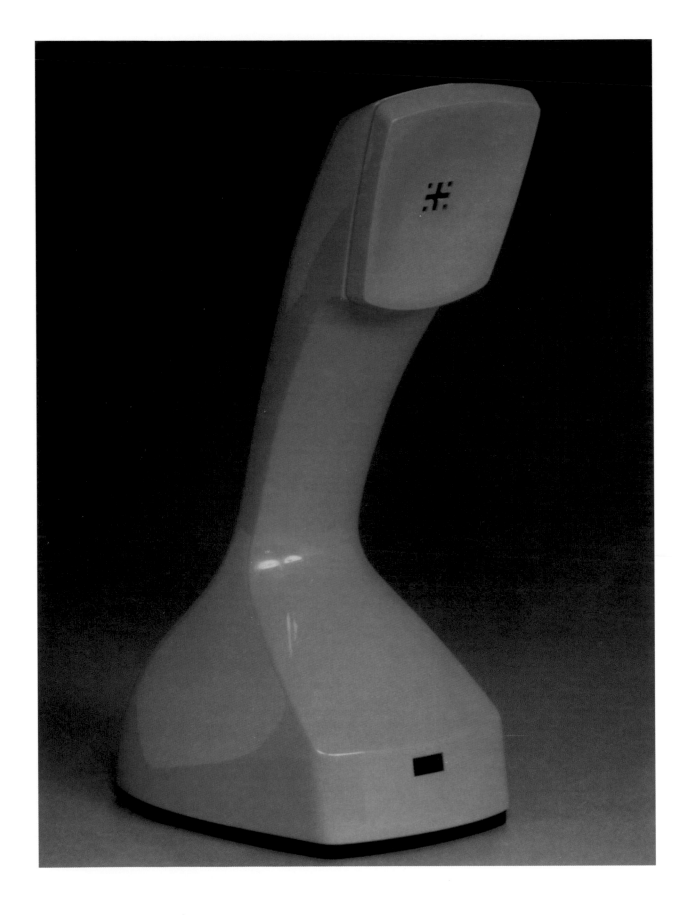

Akari Lamp

Isamu Noguchi

Isamu Noguchi was a rare combination of sculptor and garden, interior, and theater designer. His underlying concern in all these pursuits was with light and space: space within the confines of house or theater and space in nature. These paper lamps, which he called Akari, took their inspiration from the Japanese *chochins* that hung inside and outside houses in Japan, protecting candles, diffusing their light, and marking the spaces around them. Lightweight, flexible, and cheap to make, the originals and the countless copies they inspired have become part of the language of contemporary lighting for the home.

Noguchi was born in Los Angeles of an American mother and Japanese father. He spent his childhood in Japan and returned to the United States in 1918. He visited Japan frequently and explored the life and culture of his father's country, but his relationship with his father was not close. He also studied for a time with the Romanian sculptor Constantin Brancusi in Paris, worked with American architects on buildings all over the world, and designed stage sets and sculpture for Martha Graham's New York ballet company. His sculptures in stone and wood expressed the nature of the materials and were conceived for specific courtyard or garden contexts, reminiscent of the stones in Zen gardens.

In 1951, Noguchi designed the first Akari lamp, and went on to produce a whole series that were intended as expensive limited editions—like paper sculptures—but were quickly imitated in countless less expensive forms. His lamps used the traditional *chochin* technique of a flexible frame clothed in translucent paper that was collapsible. He used wire instead of bamboo, and the paper was devised to withstand the heat of electric bulbs. The lamps' forms were sculptural: round, long and thin; square, often irregular in shape, sometimes hanging, sometimes standing on metal legs. They became, and remain, almost standard features of many homes all over the world.

Ant Bentwood Chair

Arne Jacobsen

The Ant has become one of the most popular domestic chairs of the last 50 years. It was originally designed as a lightweight, inexpensive stacking chair for the Rodovre Town Hall in Denmark. It is still found stacked in the corners of schools, town halls, and social clubs all over the world. The seat and back are molded from one piece of laminated wood, following the tradition of chairs by such designers as the Finn Alvar Aalto, the Hungarian Marcel Breuer, and the American Charles Eames. The steam-bent plywood back and seat were designed to be produced by the Danish furniture factory Fritz Hansen, and were supported by a tubular steel frame that was sometimes sheathed in plastic rather than being left bare.

The designer Arne Jacobsen started with a three-legged chair in 1953, and experimented with the shape of the back and with a four-legged version in 1957. The original was available only in a teak finish that was widely associated with Scandinavia in the 1950s, but its full color range—in turquoise, orange, and pink—now fits perfectly with modern interiors. Today the Ant is manufactured in many different versions.

Jacobsen was part of the Scandinavian design resurgence of the 1950s, and like many of his fellow architects, he designed every element of the interior of his houses. He was influenced by the visual landscape that inspired the distinctive organic forms of his work in textiles and furniture. They were immediately fashionable in England and other parts of Europe, where the simple Scandinavian aesthetic became part of mainstream modernism. By the late 1950s, he was already Denmark's most famous and prolific architect and designer—he had moved from private houses to town halls and large office buildings—and was commissioned to design St. Catherine's College, Oxford, England, in 1959. In the 1960s, his Ant chair earned its place in contemporary culture when the controversial British playwright Joe Orton and the socialite Christine Keeler, who was involved in a high-level political scandal, each posed naked on it.

1954

Stratocaster Electric Guitar

Leo Fender

Leo Fender was a musician who had a passion for both electronics and woodworking. His career began in 1938, when he opened a radio repair shop in Fullerton, California. It was here, in a shed behind the shop, that he set up K & F Manufacturing, with fellow inventor Doc Kauffman, and in 1945 produced his first electric guitar. The following year he founded the Fender Electric Instrument Co.

It was Fender's experience as both a musician and a technician that led him to work on the development of the electric guitar. The guitar is a notoriously quiet instrument, and until the successful invention of the electric guitar, only the percussion and brass instruments could make enough impact to be heard in a band. Experiments were made with sound amplification from the 1930s so that the instrument could hold its own in a band and take solos. The problem was with feedback between the sound box in the guitar and the amplification system, which caused "whistling."

Fender developed the first solid body instrument in 1947, called the Broadcaster—later known as the Telecaster—and in 1951 started work on the Stratocaster, which quickly became the preferred choice for serious electric guitarists. The guitar body was made of a single piece of wood, not hollowed, and the sound came directly from the strings to the amplifier, without a sound box, which allowed it to produce a strong sound when amplified, without feedback. Other modifications included pegs on the upper part of the head that could be tuned while playing, an asymmetric body shape, and a movable bridge that enabled the player to produce vibrato or tremolo effects. Fender made the body and neck separately, screwing them together instead of gluing them. This feature aimed to reduce stock production and costs, but it had the bonus of allowing musicians to customize their guitars with different woods for neck and body and differences of shape. Fender's Stratocaster has been associated with many of the rock music greats, and has become a musical legend in its own right.

Lounge Chair and Ottoman

Charles and Ray Eames

Lounge Chair and Ottoman

1956

Charles Eames 1907–1978
Ray Eames 1913–1988

American

The genius of Charles and Ray Eames quite simply dominated design after 1950. Their lounge chair and ottoman, originally designed as a one-off birthday present for American film director Billy Wilder, have become icons of contemporary living. Charles Eames's design career had begun in the late 1930s, when Finnish architect Eliel Saarinen invited him to become first a Fellow and then Head of experimental design at the Cranbrook Academy of Art in Michigan. It was here that he met his second wife, Ray Kaiser, a painter and founder member of the American Abstract Artists group.

The Eameses set up a practice in Los Angeles, and during World War II worked with Eliel's son Eero Saarinen on research projects for the U.S. Navy, devising leg and arm splints with techniques and materials for mass production. This experience was to prove invaluable to them when they were able to resume furniture design. The Eameses exploited technical advances in molding plywood to form seating shells and a process called "cycle welding," which allowed wood to be joined to rubber, glass, and metal. These were breakthrough techniques that advanced the processes that had started at Germany's Bauhaus design school with tubular-steel chairs. After 1944 the Eameses became virtually in-house designers for furniture manufacturer Herman Miller, which became America's most prestigious furniture company.

This chair and its matching ottoman were produced for Herman Miller and were made from four molded rosewood shells. The swivel bases are of cast aluminum, and the leather upholstery was originally black but later was also produced in tan and white. The use of such luxury materials made the chair a high-cost item compared to the Eameses' other output, which was famous for being mass-produced yet well designed, and which became standard furnishing for modern interiors of the 1940s and 1950s. The Eameses' aesthetic, organic shapes, modern materials, and techniques continue to be fashionable today and still look at home in contemporary settings.

Mini Car

Alec Issigonis

The Mini was designed as a low-budget car for cheap and cheerful urban use. The aesthetics of its styling, however, quickly turned it into a symbol of the radical free spirit of the 1960s, and met a growing demand by financially independent young people for a car that would reflect the new lifestyle of the "Swinging Sixties."

Alec Issigonis was born in Turkey and moved to Britain to train as an engineer. He joined the British firm Morris (British Motor Corporation) in 1936 and designed the legendary Morris Minor car in 1948. By the late 1950s, however, Morris wanted a small car to compete with European competitors—notably the Volkswagen Beetle and the Renault 4CV—and commissioned Issigonis to design it.

The "Mini," as it came to be known, represented a breakthrough in engineering, which was motivated by the need for a small car that would nevertheless perform impressively when it came to speed and maneuverability. Issigonis mounted the engine transversely across the body, making it line up with the valves differently from the traditional method. This was a revolutionary concept, which allowed the size of the chassis to be reduced. The interior was designed to maximize every inch of space, with "pockets" in the doors to hold small items such as books and maps, and a trunk at the back that could just hold the family's luggage or shopping. The Mini had a front-wheel drive, a boxlike shape, and although it could accommodate four people in relative comfort, it was only 10 feet (3 meters) long. As well as a Mini van, a rally car model— the Mini Cooper—was brought out in the early 1960s, which enhanced the Mini's image from that of a smart, practical car to one that joined the ranks of sports cars.

The Mini arrived at a time when car ownership was expanding dramatically. It was a small and low-priced vehicle, but its sexy image and styling ensured that it was a car people were proud to own. In 2001, a new model was launched. Still recognizable as a Mini, it has a more rounded shape in keeping with contemporary design trends.

Stacking Chair

Verner Panton

Stacking Chair

1960

Verner Panton
1926–1998

Danish

This futuristic piece was the first one-piece molded plastic chair to be designed and made. It offered a new aesthetic in terms of form, lightness, and bright color. Clearly an organic shape, it is designed to fit the human body—a concept with which the chair's designer, Verner Panton, had a life-long concern.

Panton worked in the studio of Danish designer Arne Jacobsen in the early 1950s, where he would have become familiar with Jacobsen's molded plywood Ant chair. Panton moved to Switzerland in 1955, where he set up his own studio. The attraction of producing furniture made from one-piece of molded plastic that required no assembling was obvious, and it held out the possibility of cheap mass-production. Panton visited factories in Denmark that were manufacturing strong fiberglass crash helmets and buckets. At this time the aircraft industry, in particular, was experimenting with plastics giving lightweight strength, including injection-molded plastics, which had helped to drive the technology forward.

The shape and smooth, glossy, and often brightly colored surface of Panton's chair made it a pop icon.

Although Panton's plastic chair was designed in 1960 and a mold for it was made in Denmark, the technical problems involved in its production were not solved until 1967, when it was first produced by the American furniture manufacturer Herman Miller International. The problems encountered were associated with the need for strength, especially in the cantilevered seat, and the need also for the chair not to be too thick to stack successfully.

When it finally went into production, there were many other plastic chairs on the market, mainly in Italy, but none was as structurally daring as this. Its zig-zag form can be traced back to Dutch designer Gerrit Thomas Rietveld's Red/Blue chair of 1918 and forward to British designer Tom Dixon's S chair of 1987.

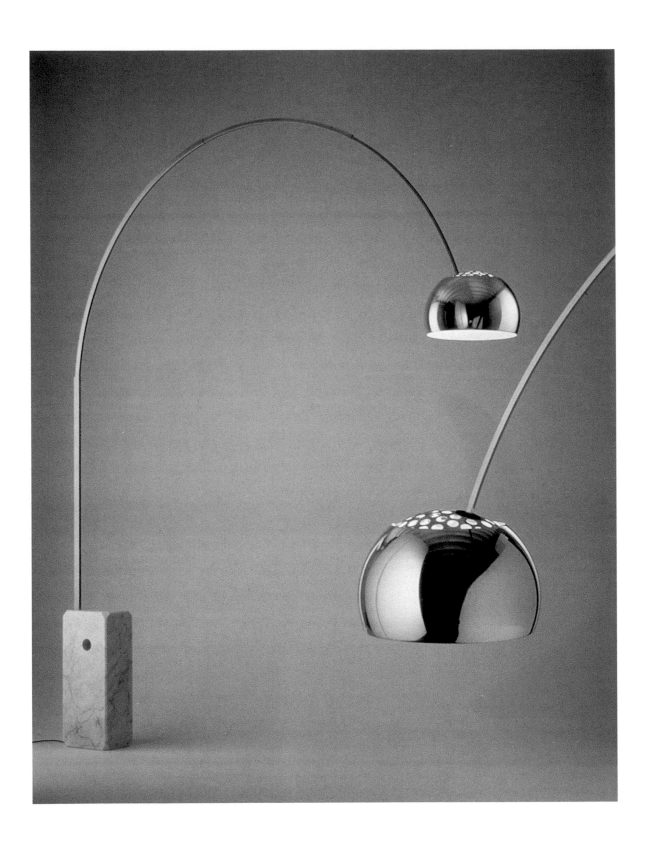

Arco Floor Lamp

Achille and Pier Giacomo Castiglioni

Arco Floor Lamp

1962

Achille Castiglioni b. 1918
Pier Giacomo Castiglioni
1913–1968

Italian

The Arco lamp was designed to light a dining table without hanging from the ceiling or being dependent on a nearby power point, but it is more usually used simply as a floor lamp for general room lighting. It has three possible heights and a hole through the heavy base that forms a handle to enable it to be moved. The juxtaposition of this slender base with the huge reach of the light creates a tension that places the lamp firmly in the postmodern period. The Arco abandoned the modernist credo of "form follows function" and the more streamlined Bauhaus objects in favor of a more radical, sculptural, and personal design vision.

The Castiglioni brothers were adventurous designers who pushed forward the technical advances that were being made at that time, and who used "ready-made" elements in their objects—famously a tractor seat for a chair in 1957—an approach inspired by the ready-made objects of the French artist Marcel Duchamp. The brothers are quoted as saying that they wanted "resonances of previous artefacts so that there is an almost ready-built relationship with the user."

The Arco lamp represents a link between the past and the present. It combines the traditional opulence of marble—a material that conjures a powerful evocation of Italy's cultural and artistic past—with the sleek, pared-down modernism of steel and polished aluminum. The Castiglioni brothers have even made a virtue of the trailing flex by cladding it in stainless steel to form an imposing arc. The Arco not only works on a practical level as a source of light, but also acts as a witty and confident piece of sculpture, defining the space which it occupies. Originally intended for use in Italian apartments, the lamp enjoyed renewed popularity in the 1990s with the vogue for loft living, which provided an opportunity to place the Arco in a large living area. It has endured as a modern classic and an icon of the post-war Italian design movement, and is still produced by the Italian company Flos.

Blow Chair

Gionatan De Pas, Donato D'Urbino, and Paolo Lomazzi

Blow Chair

1967

Gionatan De Pas
1932–1991
Donato D'Urbino b. 1935
Paolo Lomazzi b. 1936

Italian

The Blow chair has come to represent 1960s pop culture—instant, disposable, and appealing to a youthful market eager to purchase innovative products. It was also the first commercially produced inflatable chair. The technological breakthrough that made inflatable furniture possible allowed the designers to produce an amusing, surprising chair that was an instant success for Italian furniture manufacturer Zanotta, and had the added attraction of being relatively cheap.

The four architects who designed the chair had studied together in Milan during the 1960s and had concentrated on furniture design and temporary structures. They went on to design a series of inflatable buildings for the Osaka World Fair in Japan in 1970. Production of the inflatable chair was made possible by new plastics technology that used high-frequency PVC welding to seal the seams, which were under constant strain. The designers were responding to a desire at the time for furniture that had a flexible use and that was not intended to last a lifetime. Zanotta sold the chair in a flat pack for the enthusiastic purchaser to take home and blow up. Because it was vulnerable to punctures, the chair came with its own repair kit, but when it was worn out, it was happily disposed of and replaced.

The Blow chair is reminiscent of modernist chairs, especially Irish-born designer Eileen Gray's bulging Bibendum chair, which she designed for Parisian socialite Suzanne Talbot's apartment in Paris in 1933. The Blow chair became a 1960s icon, appearing in films and magazines as a statement of futuristic products that captured the imagination of the period. Once the idea of inflatable chairs had taken off, other examples produced in different shapes focused less on being furniture for the interior and more on being playthings for the bath, beach, and swimming pool. The 1980s and 1990s saw a revival of interest in inflatable designs, and companies such as the British firm Inflate produced a range of small, fun inflatables such as eggcups and keyrings.

Joe Chair

Gionatan De Pas, Donato D'Urbino, and Paolo Lomazzi

Joe Chair

1970

Gionatan De Pas
1932–1991
Donato D'Urbino b. 1935
Paolo Lomazzi b. 1936

Italian

The Joe chair is shaped like a baseball glove, and its name alludes to the New York Yankee baseball player Joe DiMaggio. The design reflected the 1960s world of pop culture and imagery that was appropriated and used for domestic design and furniture. DiMaggio's status as a national icon was assured when he married American actress Marilyn Monroe. By the time this chair appeared, she had divorced him, married American playwright Arthur Miller, and had died, in 1962, but DiMaggio's enduring fame as a sports idol lived on in the name of this chair.

The designers of the chair had established their reputation for witty contemporary pieces that caught the spirit of the age with their Blow chair, produced for Italian furniture firm Zanotta in 1967. They continued to experiment with inflatable structures and modular interchangeable designs, such as foam seating and component storage systems. The appeal of unconventional, antimodernist design that explored the themes of pop was reflected in the trio's Joe chair.

This witty piece of furniture was particularly inspired by the work of Swedish-born American sculptor Claes Oldenburg, whose superscaled images of consumer objects had attracted international attention. Oldenburg favored an art that was "political-erotical-mystical," and had produced ironic objects made from perversely chosen materials that were alarmingly out of context and scale. Oldenburg forced people to reconsider the material world round them, and invested objects with multiple meanings and disturbing juxtapositions.

The Joe chair is a practical manifestation of the spirit of the time. Although it is an object in which the function is not clearly expressed by its shape, it not only adds an irreverent touch to a room but can also work as a chair to sit on. Made of leather-upholstered polyurethane by Italian furniture company Poltronova, the Joe chair quickly became a cult object for a whole generation.

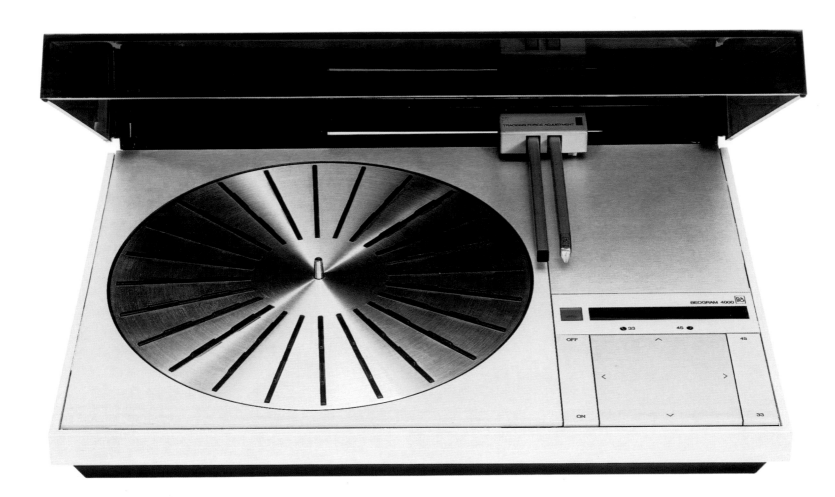

Beogram 4000

Jacob Jensen

Beogram 4000

1972

Jacob Jensen
b. 1926

Danish

In the postwar period, the dominance of Japanese sound systems and televisions was challenged by a series of products from European companies that attracted attention for the unique quality of their design and technology. The Beogram 4000, produced by the Danish electronic goods company Bang & Olufsen, is a prime example. Jacob Jensen's design for the Beogram 4000 shows significant innovation, while continuing and refining Bang & Olufsen's ethos of understatement and cohesive design.

Jensen started out as an upholsterer, later studied at the School of Applied Arts in Copenhagen, Denmark, and established himself as a designer at the office of Danish industrial designers Sigvard Bernadotte and Acton Bjørn. In 1963 he began a 30-year period with Bang & Olufsen, which had been founded in 1925. In this time Jensen designed almost every piece of audio equipment produced by Bang & Olufsen. Before Jensen's arrival the company had already begun to use top Danish designers, such as Bernadotte and Bjørn, but Jensen oversaw the creation of a unique look, establishing a coherent design vocabulary based on pure geometric space and slim-line elegance.

The Beogram's simple geometric layout is maintained whether a record is playing or not by keeping the paired arms—one that detects the size of record, the other that holds the needle—in parallel with the side of the turntable (the unit is also known as the Beogram 4000 tangential pickup). When the Beogram is started, the arms slide horizontally toward the turntable without altering their angle. The robust casing ensures that the stylus remains in contact with the record unless it is jolted forcefully. The black box is so discreet and so lacking in articulated detail that it seems as anonymous as any industrial object, and reveals as little of its designer as it does of its function. This sense of anonymity came to define the aesthetic for top-of-the-range consumer electronics. The stainless steel and aluminum surface of the turntable is offset by the wood that frames the bottom section—an easy fusion of the machine world and nature.

Tizio Table Lamp

Richard Sapper

Tizio Table Lamp

1972

Richard Sapper
b. 1932

German

When he created the Tizio table lamp for Italian furniture and lighting manufacturers Artemide, the designer Richard Sapper used the new electronic inventions of the time to create an innovative and more flexible object than the many angled work lamps that were universally in use during the 1970s. Sapper's improved engineering techniques not only make the lamp significantly lighter but also allow the articulated arms to move smoothly on snap joints, and the low-voltage halogen bulb gives a brighter, whiter light that is good to work by. The heavy transformer is located at the base of the lamp, reducing the voltage at that point and allowing the metal arms to conduct the power directly to the bulb, which eliminates the need for cumbersome housing of the flex.

Sapper was born in Munich, Germany, though he is most closely associated with Italian design. He trained as a mechanical engineer and started his career in the car-styling department of Mercedes Benz in Stuttgart, Germany. When Sapper moved to Italy in 1957, many small firms were actively seeking new design talent and employing young Italian architect-trained designers. The same was also true of large companies such as Olivetti, which also had the advantage of in-house research departments. Sapper's engineering ingenuity has been used in many design classics produced by enterprising Italian firms throughout the 20th century. His designs expressed the technological function of the object, and he worked on a large variety of products, including innovative audiovisual equipment for the pioneering Italian firm Brionvega.

This delicate lamp is finished in matt black aluminum. The thin, articulated arms have red points at the pivotal joints, and can be safely placed in any position with the head focusing a concentrated light source. The halogen bulb gives a more tranquil light than the traditional bulb, but it does get extremely hot, which makes its flexible positioning crucial. The Tizio lamp was a best-selling design for Artemide, and in 1979 it won the Compasso d'Oro—Italy's oldest and most prestigious design award.

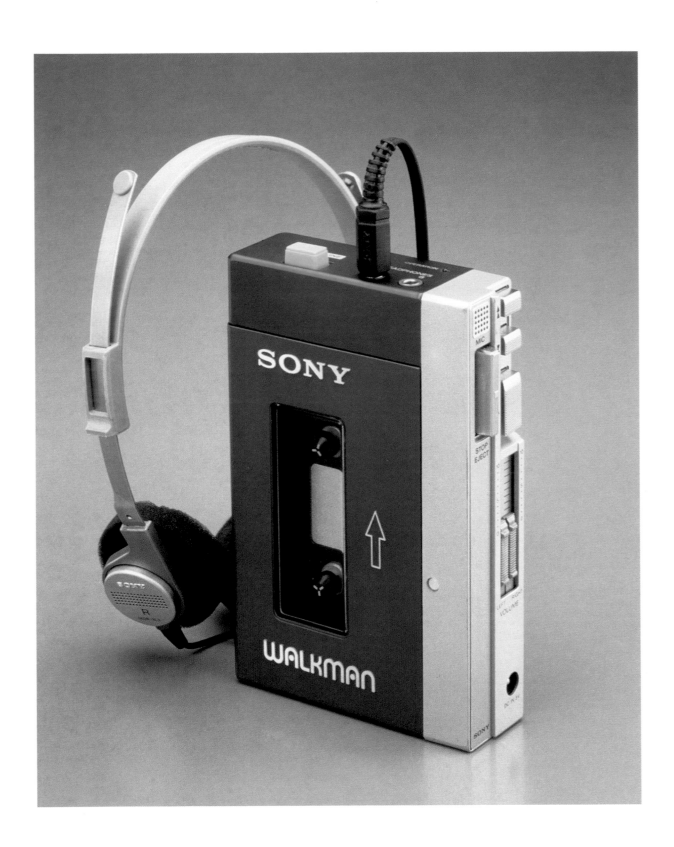

Walkman Portable Cassette Player

Sony Design Center

Walkman Portable Cassette
Player

1978

Sony Design Center

Japanese

The Walkman portable cassette player was one of the first personalized products that enabled people to create their own space and ambience in the overcrowded world in which they traveled and worked. Japanese company Sony's sales soon topped 50 million, and many different versions of the Walkman were developed, including one specifically for sports. Today the streets and public transport are full of people absorbed in their personal music, although now audiotapes are more usually replaced with CDs.

In 1958 the Tokyo Tsushin Kogyo company (Tokyo Telecommunications Engineering Corporation)—or "Totsuko"—officially changed its name to Sony. The new name came from the Latin *sonus*, meaning sound, and was consciously chosen to have an international appeal. Similarly, the name "Walkman" was chosen with the global consumer in mind and was well targeted.

Faced with declining sales in an overloaded electronics market, Sony took the exceedingly bold step of creating a new product that was a simplification of an existing one. Listening to music has always been a social activity, done with friends at home or in a concert audience. However, the chairman of Sony, Akio Morita, is reputed to have thought of inventing a portable stereophonic cassette player while he was playing tennis. The idea was initially received with some skepticism, but some ingenious marketing, spurred on by Morita's enthusiasm, persuaded people that they needed a tape player that could only be listened to by one person with headphones.

For the Walkman to work successfully, Sony needed to separate the function of listening to tapes from that of recording them. The component parts had to be solidly made as well as portable, and the earphones—previously cumbersome objects—were simplified and made light. The styling made the Walkman look functional and colorful, and it soon became a fashion accessory for young people. The fact that the name Walkman has now become a generic term is proof of the product's success.

1980

Braun Clock

Braun AG

Braun Clock

1980

Braun AG

German

The German company Braun has a reputation for design and functional electronic goods. Established by Max Braun in Frankfurt in 1921, it manufactured radios, but after Braun's death in 1951, it was taken over by his sons, Artur and Erwin, who increased its range of products for the postwar consumer. At this time a strong relationship was developed with the Hochschule für Gestaltung (College of Design) at Ulm in Germany.

Braun attracted to its staff distinguished designers from the Ulm college, such as the German Dieter Rams, who was senior designer for radio and gramophones. The company's design ethos was clearly defined by Max Bill, who co-founded the college. Bill, a Swiss-born architect and designer, had been a student at Germany's Bauhaus design school from 1927 to 1929. He wanted to see the rational approach to design continued, gradually replacing fine art with such subjects as mathematics and ergonomics. He wrote in 1949 that the form of an object should be "a harmonious expression of the sum of its function… What we specifically perceive as form, and therefore as beauty, is the natural, self-evident, and functional appearance."

Braun's electrical products included household appliances such as food mixers, a series of shavers, and photographic equipment; clocks, watches, lighters, and calculators were added in 1966. The designs are characterized by simple, undecorated forms with no use of color. The objects perform consistently to a high standard, and their aesthetic strength lies in the beguiling shapes that manage to be both functional and beautiful.

The desk clock—a version of Braun's ABWZ1 wall clock—is one of the company's most simple designs. It has no confusing tricks: it does not use Roman numerals, its clear numbers are evenly spaced, and it has well-defined "big" and "little" hands, all contained within a simple circle, with the addition of a stand so that it can be used on a table or shelf. This understated product seems to hold its own with the challenging postmodern designs that became current later in the 20th century.

Carlton Sideboard

Ettore Sottsass

Carlton Sideboard

1981

Ettore Sottsass
b. 1917

Austrian/Italian

The Carlton sideboard, which has become a classic of Italian postmodern design, incorporates all the design elements introduced by Ettore Sottsass's Memphis Design Group—unconventional and playful forms, bright colors, and a mixture of materials and patterns. Founded by Sottsass in 1981, Memphis swiftly became a mecca for international design, attracting established young designers from Austria, Japan, Britain, and the United States, as well as from Italy.

Sottsass trained as an architect in Turin, Italy, and quickly moved into design, opening a studio in Milan in 1947. He became a consultant designer for Italian office equipment firm Olivetti from 1957, where he produced both office equipment and furniture, and in 1979 he showed work with the Italian radical design company Studio Alchimia. In 1980 he founded the Milan-based design consultancy Sottsass Associati.

Since the 1970s, radical design in Italy had been moving away from the modernist dictum of "form follows function" toward a new approach. This re-examined the way things worked and produced objects that had popular and emotional appeal. The trend was facilitated by the developments in plastic and wood laminates that made bright as well as subtle colors possible, and by computer-generated abstract patterns. Sottsass studied the new techniques, wrote and lectured on his design theories, and produced a series of original pieces for Memphis. His inspiration drew on eclectic sources, ranging from traditional Indian forms to the popular culture of 1950s America and the fashion and music of London in the "Swinging Sixties."

The Carlton sideboard reflects these influences, and is provocative and radical in its design. Its shelves slope in all directions, yet it retains an overall geometric shape reminiscent of an ancient Egyptian gateway or a 20th-century robot. Its challenging form is enlivened by bright colors and by a computer-generated pattern on its base. It can be used as a room divider, sideboard, or shelving unit with added drawers.

Dyson Dual Cyclone Vacuum Cleaner

James Dyson

Dyson Dual Cyclone
Vacuum Cleaner

1983

James Dyson
b. 1947

British

Inventor and entrepreneur James Dyson has become something of a legendary figure in British design. Against the odds, he succeeded in bringing his design for a bagless vacuum cleaner to mass production. Dyson spent five years, between 1979 and 1984, building over 5000 prototypes and trying unsuccessfully to sell his idea to American and European manufacturers. He was eventually contacted by a small Japanese company that had seen a picture of the Dual Cyclone prototype on a 1983 magazine cover. In 1985—on the point of bankruptcy—Dyson struck a deal with the Japanese. But it was not until 1993, eight years later, that he was able to start manufacturing in Britain under his own name. Even then, the product was a risky one. By placing his invention at the top of the price range, Dyson gambled on the public's desire to have the best design, regardless of cost. Within months, the Dual Cyclone was outselling its rivals.

With its unconventional styling, bright colors, and highly inventive use of existing technology, Dyson's bagless vacuum cleaner revolutionized the industry. Its major advantage over other models is that it maintains constant suction. Previous vacuum cleaners relied on air being sucked through a bag. As soon as dust entered the bag, it began to clog the pores in the lining and suction was reduced. Dyson believed that the way to improve suction would be with a clogless filter. He found his inspiration in the 30-foot (9-meter) cyclone tower, used industrially to remove harmful particles from the air by centrifugal force, and applied this principle on a much smaller scale.

The Dual Cyclone boasts a number of other features that set it apart from other models. The clear bin is the result of Dyson's conviction that people would be as fascinated by the spectacle of dust being sucked up as he was. More importantly, it is obvious when the bin needs emptying. The body, made from durable ABS (a lightweight plastic) and polycarbonate, is the color of machined aluminum and a bold yellow, thereby suggesting high performance combined with a sense of fun.

Swatch Watch

Swatch

The Swatch watch is an integrated plastic watch with built-in movement that makes it impossible to repair, so making the watch, a previously valuable object, into a throwaway item. This model, Black Magic (GM101), is from the first collection of 1983.

After World War II, quartz was gradually being introduced into watches. However, the Swiss watchmaking industry was built on its precision mechanical watches, and it was reluctant to move comprehensively to the new quartz technology, which would destroy the dominance it had in precision engineering. The early quartz watches had problems with a short battery life, and LED (light-emitting diode) watches required push buttons to display the time. Solutions were found to these deficiencies with LCD (liquid crystal display) and improved battery life.

By the 1970s the new technology was being pursued in the United States and Japan, and the Swiss watchmaking industry was falling behind. A consortium of Swiss watchmakers enlisted Czech-born entrepreneur Nicolas Hayek to help reverse their ailing fortunes. Hayek's research showed that to beat the competition they would have to come up with a product that was not only well-made, tough, and analogical (with minute and second hands), but also inexpensive. Hayek bought out the consortium and set up a specialist team which, in 1981, produced the prototype of the Swatch—from "Swiss" and "watch." With 51 plastic components instead of the usual 151, the new watch cost much less to produce and assemble. Its low price, the fact that it could not be repaired, and design and color variations in the basic face and strap made a reality of a revolutionary concept—that of the watch as a throwaway fashion item.

Today the Swatch watch exists in three versions: the classic slim models in sober colors and styles; the fashion watches that are launched in seasons, like haute couture; and limited editions in precious metals. Swatch is now the world's largest manufacturer of finished watches, having sold over 200 million by the end of the 20th century.

Wedge Typewriter

Mario Bellini

Wedge Typewriter

1985–1986

Mario Bellini b.1935

Italian

Traditionally, Italian designers train first as architects, and it seems obvious that Mario Bellini, who designed this typewriter, was an architect—albeit one who was heavily engaged in industrial and furniture design (there is a sketch for this typewriter that makes it look just like an Expressionist building). Bellini graduated as an architect in 1959 from the Politecnico di Milano in Milan, and from 1961 to 1963 he was design director at La Rinascente, an Italian department store chain. In 1963, he took up a post as a consultant to the Italian office equipment firm Olivetti, and went on to design 134 office machines for it and other Italian industrial design firms, many of which won prizes. He was also engaged in designing furniture classics for the Italian firms Cassina, Vitra, and B & B Italia, and later took part in architectural projects such as the extension to the Fiera di Milano Portello and the refurbishment of the National Gallery of Victoria in Melbourne, Australia.

At the time of Bellini's appointment to Olivetti, design in Italy was flourishing, especially in small radical firms such as Archizoom and Superstudio. The large industrial companies, such as Olivetti, gave their designers secure retainer fees with freedom to experiment. They prided themselves on encouraging new talent, treating their designers like artists but giving them the necessary engineering and marketing backup.

In his analysis of the function of a typewriter, Bellini looked at the way scribes had written on a slanted surface, and lessons were read on slanting lecterns, so that reading and writing were possible together without moving the head. The same slanting angles can be seen in the Wedge typewriter. When it was introduced in the 1980s—well before the widespread use of computers made typewriters largely redundant—it was a techological and design breakthrough. With its slab-like, sculptural shape, it was not only one of the first electronic portable typewriters with a fast printing speed, but it also demonstrated that office equipment could be as stylish as furniture and fashion.

141

Whistling Kettle

Michael Graves

Whistling Kettle

1985

Michael Graves
b. 1934

American

In 1983 the Italian company Alessi had produced a singing kettle designed by German-born designer Richard Sapper. A couple of years later it was looking for a new model to succeed and complement the earlier one, but wanted it to be cheaper to produce and specifically aimed at the American mass market. Michael Graves was sympathetic to this concept and was chosen to produce the new design.

Graves studied architecture at Harvard at a time when many modernist European emigré architects, such as the Germans Walter Gropius and Erich Mendelsohn, were teaching in the United States. He has taught at Princeton since 1962, and though he has few built works, he was part of a group of East Coast architects who were experimenting with what has become known as a postmodern style—one that has had a huge influence on architecture since the 1970s. Rejecting modernism as too purist and inaccessible to the mass of people, postmodernism mixes different design styles from different eras and—in a spirit of pastiche and playfulness—unashamedly combines the élitist with the populist. One early example of Graves' architectural output, dating from 1969, was his Benacerraf House—a pavilion attached to a house in Princeton. It is a white building with touches of red and blue and clearly alludes to the 1925 Schröder House of Danish architect Gerrit Rietveld, with the elements rearranged.

For his whistling kettle, Graves used standard production methods. The appeal of the design lies in its restrained but effective use of pattern and color, as well as the irresistible bird whistle. The line of raised dots on the steel body emphasizes the conical base, and the red bead accents at each end of the blue polyamide handle echo the red molded bird mounted on the spout, which sings when the water boils. It was one of the first domestic postmodernist objects. Its price remains high, but it has sold consistently well over the years as an item of high design that stands out among kitchenware in stores and in kitchens—as well as being fun to use.

1986

"How High The Moon" Armchair

Shiro Kuramata

"How High The Moon"

1986

Shiro Kuramata
1934–1991

Japanese

By the 1970s and 1980s Japanese design had developed a new confidence and distinctive voice. The economy was booming and a resurgence of design was taking place in many spheres, including graphics and electronic consumer goods, spurred on by such companies as Sony and National Panasonic. Where previously Western ideas had been simply copied and adapted, Japanese architects and furniture designers were now producing buildings and furniture with a more original vision. National culture and aesthetics were being reinterpreted for the modern age, generating a new style that was clearly minimalist but still adhered to the traditional attention to craftsmanship and detail. The work of Shiro Kuramata and his fellow avant-garde Japanese designers, such as Kiro Kurakawa and Arata Isosaki, exemplified this new approach, and their designs for boutiques for successful Japanese designers such as the fashion designer Issey Miyake brought them worldwide recognition.

Kuramata had begun his career with a traditional training in woodcraft at the Tokyo Municipal Polytechnic High School in the late 1950s, and then at the Department of Living Design at the Kuwazawa Institute of Design, which he attended while working part-time at a furniture factory. He subsequently joined the design department of Matsuya Department Store before setting up his own design office in Tokyo in 1965.

In the 1970s he attracted international attention with his "Furniture in Irregular Forms"—a series of increasingly bold and original pieces. He also explored the potential of modern materials such as metal mesh, steel rod, aluminum, and acrylic to create an illusion of weightlessness. In his "How High the Moon" chair, made in 1986 by the Terada Tekkojo company, the see-through material from which it is constructed—nickel-plated steel mesh—is a surprise element in the design, in marked contrast to the bulk of its three-dimensional form. Kuramata's innovative use of unconventional materials in pieces such as this is one of his greatest contributions to contemporary design.

145

Royalton Hotel Bar Stool

Philippe Starck

Royalton Hotel Bar Stool

1988

Philippe Starck
b. 1949

French

Hotel interiors have created opportunities for some of the most avant-garde experiments in furniture, fittings, and interior design, and have provided consistently stimulating projects for French designer Philippe Starck. Most of Starck's startlingly original furniture and fittings are found in hotels, and he can be held responsible for the new positioning of the hotel as a place to experience the new and the contemporary. This is a concept that has spread to every major city in the world, and Starck-designed hotels, cafés, and nightclubs in Paris, Tokyo, London, Hong Kong, and New York attract style-conscious individuals seeking fashionable places to congregate.

In 1982 Starck made his first international impact with his interior design for French President François Mitterand's apartment at the Élysée Palace. All the furniture elements designed by him for the apartment were later produced independently, and their originality was recognized and successfully marketed all over the world.

The Royalton in New York was one of Starck's early hotel interiors, dating from 1988, and he was able to design and conceptualize every aspect. Every detail of the flooring, lighting, washrooms, and restaurants—right down to the hooks on the doors— was rethought. It was to be not only a state-of-the-art interior, but also a meeting place for design cognoscente with none of the elements traditionally associated with hotel groups. For instance, the reception desk and business foyer were abolished in favor of a casual arrangement of informal seating, stools, and chairs, with different levels defining spaces, making this a place to see and be seen in.

This bar stool is one of the characteristically witty pieces in the Royalton. Its legs— curvaceously plump at the top tapering to a stiletto-heel point at the bottom—create a sculptural tension with the more conventional seat, while the ingenious footrests reinforce the flowing line. The design assumes a certain youth and agility from the occupier, reaffirming the Royalton's status as a venue for the hip and fashionable.

Nintendo Game Boy

Gunpei Yokoi

Nintendo Game Boy

1989

Gunpei Yokoi
1941–1997

Japanese

The introduction of hand-held games consoles was one of the marketing success stories of the 1980s, the Nintendo Game Boy being the most successful of all. It was aimed mainly at teenage boys, offering them the opportunity for portable play, but soon developed an almost universal appeal.

Gunpei Yokoi, the inventor of the Game Boy, grew up in Kyoto, where he graduated from college with a degree in electronics, and was taken on by the Nintendo company, then a playing card manufacturer, to maintain the assembly line machinery. In 1963 Nintendo began to produce games, and in 1970 Yokoi was assigned to the games department, where he became Project Manager.

There had been a number of hand-held video game units on the market before Game Boy's release. Many of these were made by Nintendo, including its famous Game & Watch Donkey Kong product. This, however, provided only one game that was hand-wired into the console. Home consoles, on the other hand, offered a greater variety of games, but were bulky and needed mains power and a television. Yokoi's Game Boy combined the best of both these systems, offering a range of games in a hand-held unit. Being technologically simple, it was also inexpensive. Game Boy marked Nintendo's big push to capitalize on the trend for portability started by Sony's Walkman in 1978, and such was its success that it created a whole new market where none had existed before. In the first two weeks after its launch, Japanese sales reached 200,000, and by 1992 more than 32 million systems had been sold worldwide.

Today more than 700 games are available for the Game Boy, and come in single cartridges that slot easily into the back of the unit. The graphics, originally in monochrome, are now in color, and the system also boasts stereo sound. Tragically, having left Nintendo in 1996 to set up his own company, Yokoi was killed in a car accident the following year, at the age of only 56.

Balzac Chair

Matthew Hilton

Balzac Chair

1990–1991

Matthew Hilton
b. 1957

British

Matthew Hilton's Balzac chair is a reinvention of the traditional gentleman's club chair. Its sculptural lines and deep seat distinguish it from its predecessors. When it was first shown at the Milan Furniture Fair in 1991, British designer and entrepreneur Terence Conran declared it to be the best upholstered furniture design he had seen for years.

Hilton trained at Kingston Polytechnic in London and started his career making organic-looking metal objects such as candlesticks and bowls in cast aluminum. He kept control of the production process, creating the models in wood or building them with fiberglass. The objects were produced in small batches and sold well.

In the mid-1980s, Hilton's work came to the attention of Sheridan Coakley, who was running a furniture shop in London called SCP, which then specialized in 1930s tubular-steel furniture. Coakley was commissioning new, young British designers and took on Jasper Morrison and Matthew Hilton. Coakley showed Hilton's collection of tubular-steel furniture at the Milan Furniture Fair of 1986, where it was well received. Hilton's Antelope and Flipper tables, with anthropomorphic details, followed, and their flair and originality have earned them a place at London's Victoria and Albert Museum.

It was Coakley's idea to produce a version of the club chair, but at first Hilton was reluctant to move into the traditional world of upholstered furniture. However, after studying the upholstery processes used by Thetford Design in Norfolk, England, he saw the potential for a new shape and produced a chair that had "energy and movement." The chair is manufactured by two firms in Norfolk: the wooden frames in beech, with oak supporting legs, are made by Rider and Dunnett, and the upholstery is built up and covered in leather, all by hand, by Thetford Design. Originally, it was mainly designers and architects who bought the chair, but it is now a classic owned by firms and individuals who would not normally venture into modern design—there are 10 Balzac chairs in the Concorde lounge in New York's Kennedy Airport.

"Gino Zucchino" Sugar Sifters

Guido Venturini

Gino Zucchino Sugar Sifters

1993

Guido Venturini
b. 1957

Italian

Developed by the Italian firm Alessi, these sugar sifters are part of a series, or family, of "object toys" that explore the appeal of wit and humor in design. In the 1990s, Alessi felt that consumers wanted something more than good design and quality manufacturing. The object toys were part of an attempt to reject the orthodox notion of design and to engage with people, connecting the activities of doing and playing. While products need to function, they also need to be desirable and enjoyable, setting up a process of communication between the user and the object.

Alessi is a family firm that has been producing tabletop and bar-counter objects since 1921. The business has passed through three generations, and is currently directed by Alberto Alessi. It is an innovative, adventurous company that has not only commissioned many of the best-known international designers, but also has a strong historical sense. In the 1970s, Alessi revived some of the best 19th- and early 20th-century designs, such as a kettle by British designer Christopher Dresser and Bauhaus products by German designer Marianne Brandt.

Guido Venturini, who designed these anthropomorphic sugar sifters, was born in Italy in 1957 and trained as an architect in Florence. In 1985 he founded a design company named King Kong with fellow designer Stefano Giovannoni (the company was dissolved in 1989). Venturini and Giovannoni were part of a group of radical Italian designers who were practising in the 1980s, and who drew their inspiration from popular art, films, and cartoon strips. The sugar sifters that Venturini produced for Alessi are part of a series of playful domestic objects—such as cruets, kitchen containers, toilet brushes, and even toothpaste squeezers—that are available not only in galleries and designer stores but also in shopping malls. They appear in shiny metal and all the color variations that plastics can offer, with legs that simulate jumping or waddling, lids that resemble heads or hats, and handles that look like flowers or rabbit's ears.

Smart Car

DaimlerChrysler

The Smart Car is almost half the size of a normal saloon car and is designed as a two-seater city runabout. It comes in two basic models, the City Coupé and the convertible City Cabrio, and has features associated with the top end of the market, which go some way toward compensating for its small size. In 1996 the Smart Car won the European Design Prize in Maastricht in the Netherlands.

Produced in France by DaimlerChrysler with design help from Swatch, the Swiss watchmakers, and powered by a German Mercedes Benz engine, the Smart Car is an innovative vehicle that has all the advantages of a modern small car—and some other benefits too. It is highly maneuverable, has electronic fuel injection, a fully automatic gearbox or a semi-automatic one with six gears and no clutch, and offers a range of optional extras. It has a low gasoline consumption of around 57.6 miles per gallon (20.4 km per liter) and a top speed of 84 mph (135km/h). To compensate for the vulnerability of its small size, it has added safety devices including airbags and a special "safety cell" that absorbs the force of collisions. The body panels are standard and interchangeable. It is built in an ecofriendly factory, made mostly from recyclable materials, and uses a painting process that emits no solvents and produces no sludge or effluents. At the end of its life, it is almost 100 per cent recyclable.

At just over 8 feet (2.5 meters) long and 5 feet (1.5 meters) wide, perhaps the Smart Car's most attractive feature for city dwellers is that it takes up half the parking space of conventional cars. The only way this compact size can be achieved, however, is to severely restrict the cabin space. The vehicle has just two seats and a deep parcel shelf, but little room for luggage unless the passenger seat is folded back. It fulfills its objective as a short-run car, but long journeys can be uncomfortable with limited leg room. However, these features were deliberately designed to fit the Smart Car for its purpose—to be ecofriendly and to make traveling easier in overcrowded cities.

Smeg Refrigerator

Smeg

Smeg refrigerators became synonymous with designer lifestyles in the 1990s. They have become indispensable features of advertisements, films, and television programs that want to express fashionable, contemporary style.

Refrigerators have traditionally belonged to the "white goods" section of kitchen equipment. Appliances finished in white—a color that traditionally conveys cleanliness and hygiene—were designed to blend discreetly into the modern kitchen and to fit in under or next to worktops. By the 1990s, however, pressures of work on most families meant that there was less time for domestic chores. Buying groceries had to be restricted to a once-a-week expedition, and home food storage requirements changed. There was a need for a choice of refrigerator so that people with small kitchens could continue to use compact models, while those who needed greater cold storage, and who had the space, could buy larger ones.

The Italian kitchen appliance manufacturer Smeg began life as a metal enameling factory situated in the village of Guastalla in Emelia province in northern Italy—hence its name, Smalterie Metallurgiche Emiliane Guastalla, which was shortened to the acronym S.M.E.G. The company—whose motto is "technology with style"—spotted the design potential in the need for larger fridges, and introduced new models in unusual colors that declared their presence in the kitchen and added a sense of style. Although other companies also experimented with alternative designs, including the Italian firm Zanussi, the iconic appeal of the Smeg refrigerator lay in its clever appropriation of 1950s American streamlining. The rounded corners, the detailing in the handles, and the prominent branding, using a bold, sans serif typeface, all evoke the golden era of American automobile styling. The choice of colors also has strong retro appeal, ranging from old-fashioned cream to sugary pastels in pink, green, and blue, as well as more contemporary red, deep blue, and silver.

1996

Nokia Cell Phones

Nokia

Nokia Cell Phones

1996

Nokia

Finnish

Nokia is a Finnish company whose use of superior styling and state-of-the-art information technology have made it a world leader in the lucrative and ever-expanding market for cell telephones. The reliability and attractive appearance of its products continues to maintain the company's ascendancy in this highly competitive field.

Nokia started in 1865 as a wood-pulp mill in southern Finland on the banks of the River Emäkoski. The waters were used to produce hydroelectricity. Nokia had an international clientele, and a community grew up around the works. Gradually, it evolved through a Rubber Works and Cable Company to form the Nokia Group. In the early 1970s, it carried out research into semiconductor technology and developed the digital switch Nokia DX 200, which became the basis for its network infrastructure. This development coincided with new legislation from the Finnish telecommunications authority, which enabled the setting up of a mobile network for car phones connected to the public network. Following the Global System for Mobile Communications (GSM)—a common standard for digital mobile telephony—at the end of the 1980s, Nokia made agreements to supply GSM networks to European countries. By August 1997 they had supplied these to operators in 31 countries.

Nokia established their leading position early by designing excellent menus for their mobile phones that were both comprehensive and easy to use, thus creating a loyal client base. Bright, attractive casing increased the appeal of the products, which were well marketed and advertised. The addition of a large range of games to the applications proved highly popular with young users—always a key market for Nokia. The company has continued to keep pace with electronic developments: in 2000 they produced a WAP (Wireless Application Protocol) model that gave in-built Internet access, and this has been followed by many new applications including models that take pictures and will soon be able to edit them and save them to a digital photograph album.

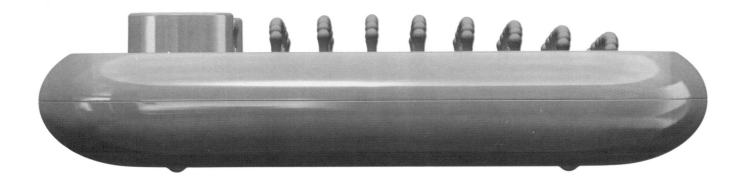

1997

Dish Doctor

Marc Newson

Dish Doctor

1997

Marc Newson
b. 1963

Australian

Marc Newson has become a designer of international reputation whose work can be seen in museums in Paris, New York, and London. His design vision has created a unique family of objects that share an individual approach. Newson has often said that one of the most important factors in his creative personality has been a life spent traveling extensively. He studied sculpture and jewelry at Sydney College of the Arts, Australia, has since lived in Japan, France, South Korea, and England, and has worked for firms in those countries and in Italy. His work covers a similarly diverse range of product and furniture design, the area in which he first made his name.

In 1991 Newson set up a studio in Paris, where he worked with European companies such as the Italian firm Cappellini and Flos, and in 1995 produced a series of interior designs for restaurants, studios, and stores in London, Cologne, Berlin, and Tokyo. In 1997 he opened a larger studio in London, where he is still based. From the relatively low-tech world of furniture design, he progressed through the rapid prototype technologies with computer-aided design (CAD) for products, and ventured into new areas with designs for a bicycle and for the interior of a small jet.

Newson's interest is not only with outward appearance but also with function and with the relationships between design, science, and nature. This dish drainer for the Italian firm Magis is a witty, colorful object in which purpose is not immediately obvious—its colors and shapes make it look more like a toy or game. The flexible pegs that hold the crockery are sometimes in two different colors that contrast with those of the base. The neat, fitted tray underneath holds the drained water and protects the surface on which the drainer rests. The peg height and positioning are ingeniously designed to hold crockery in any direction, and the two integrated holders keep the cutlery separate. Newson's Dish Doctor is an example of a radical rethink of the design of a humble domestic object that has provided a fresh, stimulating solution.

Hannibal Tape Dispenser

Julian Brown

Hannibal Tape Dispenser

1998

Julian Brown
b. 1955

British

Julian Brown studied product design at Leicester Polytechnic in England and then at London's Royal College of Art, where he graduated in 1983. His first post after graduation was in Austria with the Porsche Design Studio. He then formed his own company, Lovegrove and Brown, in London and in 1990 set up StudioBrown, an independent consultancy located in Bath, England. In 1998 he was elected a "royal designer" for industry by the Royal Society of Arts, London. He designs for several international companies such as Sony, Apple, NEC, and ACCO, producing a wide range of products, including a laptop computer and many domestic objects.

This tape dispenser was commissioned by the Italian firm Rexite, for whom Brown had already designed a translucent alarm clock named Vertingetorige—a global best-seller. Rexite has a reputation for commissioning innovative designs for office and home accessories. Brown's brief was to design three desk accessories—a stapler, hole punch, and tape dispenser—in which the unique selling point was that they should not only be functional but should also be fun and witty. Each item was to resemble an animal—in the case of the tape dispenser, an elephant. Brown is quoted as saying "Hannibal is a product of the heart with a message of humor entwined with functionality; neither dominates but each serves to reinforce the other."

Brown made a detailed study of the basic geometry connecting the tape roll, the pulling and cutting actions, and the shell-like case. He also examined the height the cutting blade needed to be from the table to facilitate the downward pull. Once these mechanisms had been explored, the elephant shape with the tape stretching to the end of the "trunk" became apparent. The trunk has radial ribs and folds back inside the body, also with radial ribs, so that the dispenser can be closed when not in use to keep the tape dust-free. The prize-winning and highly popular Hannibal tape dispenser comes in several colorways and in translucent and opaque versions.

Collect all five.

The new iMac. Now in five flavours. . Think different.

iMac Computer

Jonathan Ive

iMac Computer

1998

Jonathan Ive
b. 1967

British

In the late 1990s, Apple Macintosh computers were struggling for a market share with IBM-compatible PCs, which sold at very competitive prices. The breakthrough came with the appointment of a new design team at Apple, led by industrial designer Jonathan Ive. Before the iMac, computers were off-white or beige boxes, surrounded by cables, that stood in offices and were seen as complex and somewhat daunting pieces of technology. Ive and his design team resolved to rethink the whole relationship of form to function, and felt that there was very little about the various operations performed by a computer that determined its shape. They resolved to make an object that would not alienate nonexperts and that would become "accessible, understandable, and almost familiar."

Their solution was to make the plastic case transparent, which shifted the emphasis from the surface to the glowing interior, and was an ingenious way of demystifying the computer. Ive also rethought other creative design details for the iMac. A handle set into the case made the computer easy to move in one piece and dispensed with the notion that it was untouchable, fragile, and precious. The final decisive factor in its success was the rich, fashionable color—first a bright blue-green and then a series of fruity colors that were chosen to appeal to contemporary tastes and decors. The new computer had instant appeal, and transformed the industry and the fortunes of Apple: people bought iMacs for their homes and offices, and they were given pride of place in showrooms. Sales were also helped by an innovative and highly successful advertising campaign that positioned Apple at the cutting edge of design.

Apple brought out a series of additional products that incorporated new technology and programs, such as video editing. In 2002 the new iMac appeared, also designed by Ive, featuring a dome-shaped base and a flat screen that is adjustable for height and position. It also contains a suite of software for digital photography, music, and movies.

iBook "Notebook" Computer

Apple Design

Under the guidance of British industrial designer Jonathan Ive, Apple has become the world leader in the design of modern computers, and has turned around the market. By replacing the conventional boring beige or gray box with a series of design classics, the company has introduced the idea that personal computers can be individual, fashionable, and desirable objects not only to use but also to look at.

The original Apple iBook succeeded the iMac in 1999, joining the fast-developing range of laptop computers that enabled the user to work anywhere—on the train or aeroplane, in a hotel room, or even on the beach. The new iBook offers a range of even more sophisticated features, including 128MB of memory expandable to 640MB, 600 or 700 MHz of processing power, and up to six hours of battery life on one charge. With an additional "airport" card installed, wireless access to the Internet is possible. Even without this extra, the internal modem gives easy access to the Internet, and the iBook is designed to allow quick connection to various digital appliances. Models with a "combo" drive also enable users to burn their own music CDs.

What sets this iBook apart from its rivals, however, is not its technical capabilities, but its size. Even the larger of the two models, with its 14-inch (36-cm) screen—the smaller model has a 12-inch (30-cm) screen—is only 12¾ inches (32.3 cm) wide, 10 inches (25.9 cm) high, and 1⅜ inches (1.35 cm) thick. Offering high performance in a package not much larger than an A4 notebook, Apple's new "notebook" computer was aimed at the student market, and was marketed as being small enough to fit inside a backpack. To protect it against knocks, the casing is made of tough polycarbonate plastic. A sturdy magnesium frame gives the computer added strength, while making it lighter than other laptops. Rubber mounts make the hard drive more tolerant of bumps while it is being carried, and there are no protruding latches or levers to break off. The iBook is part of Apple's quest to revolutionize computer design and make new technology user-friendly.

Index